PART I.—INTRODUCTION.

I.—ELEMENTS OF THE ENGLISH VOCABULARY.

1. Etymology[2] is the study which treats of the derivation of words,—that is, of their structure and history.

2. English etymology, or word-analysis, treats of the derivation of English words.

3. The **vocabulary**[3] of a language is the whole body of words in that language. Hence the English vocabulary consists of all the words in the English language.

I. The complete study of any language comprises two distinct inquiries,—the study of the *grammar* of the language, and the study of its *vocabulary*. Word-analysis has to do exclusively with the vocabulary.

II. The term "etymology" as used in grammar must be carefully distinguished from "etymology" in the sense of word-analysis. Grammatical etymology treats solely of the grammatical changes in words, and does not concern itself with their derivation; historical etymology treats of the structure, composition, and history of words. Thus the relation of *loves, loving, loved* to the verb *love* is a matter of grammatical etmology; but the relation of *lover, lovely,* or *loveliness* to *love* is a matter of historical etymology.

III. The English vocabulary is very extensive, as is shown by the fact that in Webster's Unabridged Dictionary there are nearly 100,000 words. But it should be observed that 3,000 or 4,000 serve all the ordinary purposes of oral and written communication. The Old Testament contains 5,642 words; Milton uses about 8,000; and Shakespeare, whose vocabulary is more extensive than that of any other English writer, employs no more than 15,000 words.

4. The **principal elements** of the English vocabulary are words of Anglo-Saxon and of Latin or *French-Latin* origin.

5. Anglo-Saxon is the earliest form of English. The whole of the grammar of our language, and the most largely used part of its vocabulary, are Anglo-Saxon.

I. Anglo-Saxon belongs to the Low German[4] division of the Teutonic stock of languages. Its relations to the other languages of Europe—all of which are classed together as the Aryan, or Indo-European family of languages—may be seen from the following table:—

Indo-European Family.	CELTIC STOCK			as Welsh, Gaelic.
	SLAVONIC STOCK			as Russian.
	CLASSIC STOCK	Greek		
		Latin	Italian. Spanish. French, etc.	
	TEUTONIC STOCK	Scandinavian:		as Swedish.
		German	High	as Modern

				Ger.:	German.
				Low Ger.:	as Anglo-Saxon.

II. The term "Anglo-Saxon" is derived from the names *Angles* and *Saxons*, two North German tribes who, in the fifth century A.D., invaded Britain, conquered the native Britons, and possessed themselves of the land, which they called England, that is, Angle-land. The Britons spoke a Celtic language, best represented by modern Welsh. Some British words were adopted into Anglo-Saxon, and still continue in our language.

6. The **Latin** element in the English vocabulary consists of a large number of words of Latin origin, adopted directly into English at various periods.

The principal periods, during which Latin words were brought directly into English are:—

1. At the introduction of Christianity into England by the Latin Catholic missionaries, A.D. 596.

2. At the revival of classical learning in the sixteenth century.

3. By modern writers.

7. The **French-Latin** element in the English language consists of French words, first largely introduced into English by the Norman-French who conquered England in the eleventh century, A.D.

I. French, like Italian, Spanish, and Portuguese, is substantially Latin, but Latin considerably altered by loss of grammatical forms and by other changes. This language the Norman-French invaders brought with them into England, and they continued to use it for more than two centuries after the Conquest. Yet, as they were not so numerous as the native population, the old Anglo-Saxon finally prevailed, though with an immense infusion of French words.

II. French-Latin words—that is, Latin words introduced through the French—can often be readily distinguished by their being more changed in form than the Latin terms directly introduced into our language. Thus—

Latin.	**French.**	**English.**
inimi'cus	ennemi	enemy
pop'ulus	peuple	people
se'nior	sire	sir

8. Other Elements.—In addition to its primary constituents—namely, the Anglo-Saxon, Latin, and French-Latin—the English vocabulary contains a large number of Greek derivatives and a considerable number of Italian, Spanish, and Portuguese words, besides various terms derived from miscellaneous sources.

The following are examples of words taken from miscellaneous sources; that is, from sources other than Anglo-Saxon, Latin, French-Latin, and Greek:—

Hebrew: amen, cherub, jubilee, leviathan, manna, sabbath, seraph.

Arabic: admiral, alcohol, algebra, assassin, camphor, caravan, chemistry, cipher, coffee, elixir, gazelle, lemon, magazine, nabob, sultan.

Turkish: bey, chibouk, chouse, janissary, kiosk, tulip.

Persian: azure, bazaar, checkmate, chess, cimeter, demijohn, dervise, orange, paradise, pasha, turban.

Hindustani: calico, jungle, pariah, punch, rupee, shampoo, toddy.

Malay: a-muck, bamboo, bantam, gamboge, gong, gutta-percha, mango.

Chinese: nankeen, tea.

Polynesian: kangaroo, taboo, tattoo.

American Indian: maize, moccasin, pemmican, potato, tobacco, tomahawk, tomato, wigwam.

Celtic: bard, bran, brat, cradle, clan, druid, pony, whiskey.

Scandinavian: by-law, clown, dregs, fellow, glade, hustings, kidnap, plough.

Dutch, or Hollandish: block, boom, bowsprit, reef, skates, sloop, yacht.

Italian: canto, cupola, gondola, grotto, lava, opera, piano, regatta, soprano, stucco, vista.

Spanish: armada, cargo, cigar, desperado, flotilla, grandee, mosquito, mulatto, punctilio, sherry, sierra.

Portuguese: caste, commodore, fetish, mandarin, palaver.

9. Proportions.—On an examination of passages selected from modern English authors, it is found that of every hundred words sixty are of Anglo-Saxon origin, thirty of Latin, five of Greek, and all the other sources combined furnish the remaining five.

By actual count, there are more words of classical than of Anglo-Saxon origin in the English vocabulary,—probably two and a half times as many of the former as of the latter. But Anglo-Saxon words are so much more employed—owing to the constant repetition of conjunctions, prepositions, adverbs, auxiliaries, etc. (all of Anglo-Saxon origin)—that in any page of even the most Latinized writer they greatly preponderate. In the Bible, and in Shakespeare's vocabulary, they are in the proportion of ninety per cent. For specimens showing Anglo-Saxon words, see p. 136.

II.—ETYMOLOGICAL CLASSES OF WORDS.

10. Classes by Origin.—With respect to their origin, words are divided into two classes,—primitive words and derivative words.

11. A **primitive** word, or root, is one that cannot be reduced to a more simple form in the language to which it is native: as, *man, good, run.*

12. A **derivative** word is one made up of a root and one or more *formative elements*: as, man*ly*, good*ness*, run*ner*.

The formative elements are called prefixes and suffixes. (See §§ 16, 17.)

13. By Composition.—With respect to their composition, words are divided into two classes,—simple and compound words.

14. A **simple** word consists of a single significant term: as, *school, master, rain, bow.*

15. A **compound** word is one made up of two or more simple words united: as, *school-master, rainbow.*

In some compound words the constituent parts are joined by the hyphen as *school-master;* in others the parts coalesce and the compound forms a single (though not a *simple*) word, as *rainbow.*

III.—PREFIXES AND SUFFIXES.

16. A prefix is a significant syllable or word placed before and joined with a word to modify its meaning: as, unsafe = *not* safe; remove = move *back*; circumnavigate = sail *around*.

17. A suffix is a significant syllable or syllables placed after and joined with a word to modify its meaning: as, safe**ly** = in a safe *manner*; mov**able** = that may be moved; nav**igation** = *act* of sailing.

The word *affix* signifies either a prefix or a suffix; and the verb *to affix* means to join a prefix or a suffix to a root-word.

EXERCISE.

Tell whether the following words are primitive or derivative, and also whether simple or compound:—

1 grace
2 sign
3 design
4 midshipman
5 wash
6 sea
7 workman
8 love
9 lovely
10 white
11 childhood
12 kingdom
13 rub
14 music
15 musician
16 music-teacher
17 footstep
18 glad
19 redness
20 school
21 fire
22 watch-key
23 give
24 forget

Final *e* of a primitive word is dropped on taking a suffix beginning with a vowel: as, blame + able = blamable; guide + ance = guidance; come + ing = coming; force + ible = forcible; obscure + ity = obscurity.

> **Exception 1.**—Words ending in *ge* or *ce* usually retain the *e* before a suffix beginning with *a* or *o*, for the reason that *c* and *g* would have the hard sound if the *e* were dropped: as, peace + able = peaceable; change + able = changeable; courage + ous = courageous.

> **Exception 2.**—Words ending in *oe* retain the *e* to preserve the sound of the root: as, shoe + ing = shoeing; hoe + ing = hoeing. The *e* is retained in a few words to prevent their being confounded with similar words: as, singe + ing = singeing (to prevent its being confounded with singing).

Rule II.—*Final "e" followed by a Consonant.*

Final *e* of a primitive word is retained on taking a suffix beginning with a consonant: as, pale + ness = paleness; large + ly = largely.

> **Exception 1.**—When the final *e* is preceded by a vowel, it is sometimes omitted; as, due + ly = duly; true + ly = truly; whole + ly = wholly.

> **Exception 2.**—A few words ending in *e* drop the *e* before a suffix beginning with a consonant: as, judge + ment = judgment; lodge + ment = lodgment; abridge + ment = abridgment.

Rule III.—*Final "y" preceded by a Consonant.*

Final *y* of a primitive word, when preceded by a consonant, is generally changed into *i* on the addition of a suffix.

> **Exception 1.**—Before *ing* or *ish*, the final *y* is retained to prevent the doubling of the *i*: as, pity + ing = pitying.

> **Exception 2.**—Words ending in *ie* and dropping the *e*, by Rule I. change the *i* into *y* to prevent the doubling of the *i*: as, die + ing = dying; lie + ing = lying.

> **Exception 3.**—Final *y* is sometimes changed into *e*: as, duty + ous = duteous; beauty + ous = beauteous.

Rule IV.—*Final "y" preceded by a Vowel.*

Final *y* of a primitive word, when preceded by a vowel, should not be changed into an *i* before a suffix: as, joy + less = joyless.

Rule V.—*Doubling.*

Monosyllables and other words accented on the last syllable, when they end with a single consonant, preceded by a single vowel, or by a vowel after *qu*, double their final letter before a suffix beginning with a vowel: as, rob + ed = robbed; fop + ish = foppish; squat + er = squatter; prefer' + ing = prefer'ring.

> **Exceptions.**—*X* final, being equivalent to *ks*, is never doubled; and when the derivative does not retain the accent of the root, the final consonant is not always doubled: as, prefer' + ence = pref'erence.

PART II.—THE LATIN ELEMENT.

I.—LATIN PREFIXES.

Prefix.	Signification.	Example.	Definition.
a-		a-vert	to turn *from*.
ab-	= *from*	ab-solve	to release *from*.
abs-		abs-tain	to hold *from*.
ad-		ad-here	to stick *to*.
a-		a-gree	to be pleasing *to*.
ac-		ac-cede	to yield *to*.
af-		af-fix	to fix *to*.
ag-	= *to*	ag-grieve	to give pain *to*.
al-		al-ly	to bind *to*.
an-		an-nex	to tie *to*.
ap-		ap-pend	to hang *to*.
ar-		ar-rive	to reach *to*.
as-		as-sent	to yield *to*.

NOTE.—The forms **ac-**, **af-**, etc., are euphonic variations of **ad-**, and follow generally the rule that the final consonant of the prefix assimilates to the initial letter of the root.

am-	= *around*	am-putate	to cut *around*.
amb-		amb-ient	going *around*.
ante-	= *before*	ante-cedent	going *before*.
anti-		anti-cipate	to take *before*.
bi-	= *two* or	bi-ped	a *two*-footed animal.
bis-	*twice*	bis-cuit	*twice* cooked.

circum-	= *around*	circum-navigate	to sail *around*.
circu-		circu-it	journey *around*.

con-		con-vene	to come *together*.
co-		co-equal	equal *with*.
co-	= *with* or	co-gnate	born *together*.
col-	*together*	col-loquy	a speaking *with* another.
com-		com-pose	to put *together*.
cor-		cor-relative	relative *with*.

NOTE.—The forms **co-, col-, com-**, and **cor-**, are euphonic variations of **con-**.

contra-		contra-dict	to speak *against*
contro-	= *against*	contro-vert	to turn *against*
counter-		counter-mand	to order *against*

de-	= *down* or *off*	de-pose; de-fend	to put *down*; fend *off*.

dis-	*asunder*	dis-pel	to drive *asunder*.
di-	= *apart*	di-vert	to turn *apart*.
dif-	*opposite of*	dif-fer	to bear *apart*; disagree.

NOTE.—The forms **di-** and **dif-** are euphonic forms of **dis-**; **dif-** is used before a root beginning with a vowel.

ex-		ex-clude	to shut *out*.
e-		e-ject	to cast *out*.
ec-	= *out* or *from*	ec-centric	*from* the center.
ef-		ef-flux	a flowing *out*.

NOTE.—**e-**, **ec-**, and **ef-** are euphonic variations of **ex-**. When prefixed to the name of an office, **ex-** denotes that the person formerly held the office named: as, *ex*-mayor, the former mayor.

extra-	= *beyond*	extra-ordinary	*beyond* ordinary.

in-		in-clude	to shut *in*.
il-	(in nouns and	il-luminate	to throw light *on*.
im-	verbs)	im-port	to carry *in*.
ir-	= *in, into, on*	ir-rigate	to pour water *on*.
en-, em-		en-force	to force *on*.

NOTE.—The forms **il-**, **im-**, and **ir-** are euphonic variations of **in-**. The forms **en-** and **em-** are of French origin.

in-		in-sane	*not* sane.
i(n)	(in adjectives	i-gnoble	*not* noble.
il-	and nouns.)	il-legal	*not* legal.
im-	= *not*	im-mature	*not* mature.
ir-		ir-regular	*not* regular.

inter-	= *between* or	inter-cede	to go *between*.
intel-	*among*	intel-ligent	choosing *between*.

intra-	= *inside of*	intra-mural	*inside of* the walls.

intro-	= *within, into*	intro-duce	to lead *into*

juxta-	= *near*	juxta-position	a placing *near*

non-	= *not*	non-combatant	*not* fighting.

NOTE.—A hyphen is generally, though not always, placed between *non-* and the root.

ob-	*in the way*,	ob-ject	to throw *against*.
o-	= *against*,	o-mit	to leave *out*.
oc-	or *out*	oc-cur	to run *against*;

			hence, to happen.
of-		of-fend	to strike *against*.
op-		op-pose	to put one's self *against*.
per-	= *through,*	per-vade;	to pass *through*;
pel-	*thoroughly*	per-fect	*thoroughly* made.
		pel-lucid	*thoroughly* clear.

NOTE.—Standing alone, **per-** signifies *by*: as, *per annum, by* the year.

post-	= *after, behind*	post-script	written *after*.
pre-	= *before*	pre-cede	to go *before*.
preter-	= *beyond*	preter-natural	*beyond* nature.
pro	= *for, forth,* or *forward*	pro-noun / pro-pose	*for* a noun. / to put *forth*.

NOTE.—In a few instances **pro-** is changed into **pur-**, as *pur*pose; into **por-**, as *por*tray; and into **pol-**, as *pol*lute.

re-	= *back* or	re-pel	to drive *back*.
red-	*anew*	red-eem	to buy *back*.
retro-	= *backwards*	retro-grade	going *backwards*.
se-	= *aside, apart*	se-cede	to go *apart*.
sine-	= *without*	sine-cure	*without* care.

sub-	= *under* or	sub-scribe	to write *under*.
suc-	*after*	suc-ceed	to follow *after*.
suf-		suf-fer	to *undergo*.
sug-		sug-gest	to bring to mind from *under*.
sum-		sum-mon	
sup-		sup-port	to hint from *under*.
sus-		sus-tain	to bear by being *under*.
			to *under*-hold.

NOTE.—The euphonic variations **suc-**, **suf-**, **sug-**, **sum-**, **sup-**, result from assimilating the *b* of **sub-** to the initial letter of the root. In "sustain" **sus-** is a contraction of *subs-* for *sub-*.

subter-	= *under* or *beneath*	subter-fuge	a flying *under*.

super-	= *above* or *over*	super-natural	*above* nature.
		super-vise	to *over*-see.

NOTE.—In derivatives through the French, **super-** takes the form **sur-**, as *sur*-vey, to look over.

trans- tra-	= *through*, *over*, or *beyond*	trans-gress tra-verse	to step *beyond*. to pass *over*.

ultra-	= *beyond*, or *extremely*	ultra-montane	*beyond* the mountain (the Alps).
		ultra-conservative	*extremely* conservative.

II.—LATIN SUFFIXES.

Suffix.	Signification.	Example.	Definition.

-able -ible -ble	= *that may be*; *fit to be*	cur-able possi-ble solu-ble	*that may be* cured. *that may be* done. *that may be* dissolved.
-ac	= *relating to* *or* *resembling*	cardi-ac demoni-ac	*relating to* the heart. *like* a demon.

NOTE.—The suffix **-ac** is found only in Latin derivatives of Greek origin.

-aceous -acious	= *of;* *having the* *quality of*	sapon-aceous cap-acious	*having the quality of* soap. *having the quality of* holding much.
-acy	= *condition of* *being*; *office of*	celib-acy cur-acy	*condition of being* single. *office of* a curate.
-age	= *act,* *condition*, or *collection of*	marri-age vassal-age foli-age	*act of* marrying. *condition of* a vassal. *collection of* leaves.

NOTE.—The suffix **-age** is found only in French-Latin derivatives.

-al	adj. = *relating to* n. *the act of;* *that which*	ment-al remov-al capit-al	*relating to* the mind. *the act of* removing. *that which* forms the

Suffix	Meaning	Example	Definition
			head of a column.
-an -ane	= adj. *relating to* or *befitting* n. *one who*	hum-an hum-ane artis-an	*relating to* mankind. *befitting* a man. *one who* follows a trade.
-ance -ancy	= *state or quality of being*	vigil-ance eleg-ance	*state of being* watchful. *quality of being* elegant.
-ant	= adj. *being* n. *one who*	vigil-ant assist-ant	*being* watchful. *one who* assists.
-ar	= *relating to; like*	lun-ar circul-ar	*relating to* the moon. *like* a circle.
-ary	= adj. *relating to* n. *one who*; *place where*	epistol-ary mission-ary avi-ary	*relating to* a letter. *one who is* sent out. *a place where* birds are kept.
-ate	= n. *one who is* adj. *having the quality of* v. *to perform the act of,* or *cause*	deleg-ate accur-ate navig-ate	*one who is* sent by others. *having the quality of* accuracy. *to perform the act of* sailing.

Suffix	Meaning	Example	Definition
-cle -cule	= *minute*	vesi-cle animal-cule	a *minute* vessel. a *minute* animal.
-ee	= *one to whom*	refer-ee	*one to whom* something is referred.

NOTE.—This suffix is found only in words of French-Latin origin.

Suffix	Meaning	Example	Definition
-eer -ier	= *one who*	engin-eer brigad-ier	*one who* has charge of an engine. *one who* has charge of a brigade.

NOTE.—These suffixes are found only in words of French-Latin origin.

Suffix	Meaning	Example	Definition
-ene	= *having relation to*	terr-ene	*having relation to* the earth.
-ence -ency	= *state of being* or *quality of*	pres-ence tend-ency	*state of being* present. *quality of* tending towards.
-ent	= n. *one who* or *which* adj. *being* or *-ing*	stud-ent equival-ent	*one who* studies. *being* equal to, equal*ing*.
-escence	= *state of becoming*	conval-escence	*state of becoming* well.

-escent	= *becoming*	conval-escent	*becoming* well.
-ess	= *female*	lion-ess	a *female* lion.

NOTE.—This suffix is used only in words of French-Latin origin.

-ferous	= *producing*	coni-ferous	*producing* cones.
-fic	= *making, causing*	sopori-fic	*causing* sleep.
-fice	= *something done* or *made*	arti-fice	*something done* with art.
-fy	= *to make*	forti-fy	*to make* strong.
-ic -ical	= n. *one who* adj. *like, made of, relating to*	rust-ic hero-ic metall-ic histor-ical	*one who has countrified manners. like* a hero. *made of* metal. *relating to* history.

NOTE.—These suffixes are found only in Latin words of Greek origin, namely, adjectives in **-ikos**. In words belonging to chemistry derivatives in **-ic** denote the acid containing most oxygen, when more than one is formed: as *nitric* acid.

-ice	*that which*	just-ice	*that which* is just.
-ics -ic	*the science of*	mathemat-ics arithmet-ic	*the science of* quantity. *the science of* number.

NOTE.—These suffixes are found only in Latin words of Greek origin.

-id	= *being* or -*ing*	acr-id; flu-id	*being* bitter; flow*ing*.
-*ile*	= *relating to*; *apt for*	puer-ile docile	*relating to* a boy. *apt for* being taught.
-ine	= *relating to; like*	femin-ine alkal-ine	*relating to* a woman. *like* an alkali.
-ion	= *the act of, state of being, or -ing*	expuls-ion corrupt-ion frict-ion	*the act of* expelling. *state of being* corrupt. rubb*ing*.
-ish	= *to make*	publ-ish	*to make* public.
-ise -ize	= *to render,* or *perform the act of*	fertil-ize	*to render* fertile.

NOTE.—The suffix **-ise, -ize**, is of French origin, and is freely added to Latin roots in forming English derivatives.

-ism	= *state or act of; idiom*	hero-ism Gallic-ism	*state of* a hero. a French *idiom*.

NOTE.—This suffix, except when signifying an idiom, is found only in words of Greek origin.

-ist	one who = practices or is devoted to	art-ist botan-ist	one who practices an art. one who is devoted to botany.
-ite -yte	= n. one who is adj. being	favor-ite defin-ite prosel-yte	one who is favored. being well defined. one who is brought over.

NOTE.—The form **-yte** is found only in words of Greek origin.

-ity -ty	= state or quality of being	security ability liber-ty	state of being secure. quality of being able. state of being free.
-ive	n. one who is = or that which adj. having the power or quality	capt-ive cohes-ive	one who is taken. having power to stick.
-ix	= feminine	testatr-ix	a woman who leaves a will.
ize	(See **ise.**)		
-ment	state of being = or act of; that which	excite-ment induce-ment	state of being excited. that which induces.

-mony	*state or* = *quality of;* *that which*	matri-mony testi-mony	*state of* marriage. *that which* is testified.
-or	*one who;* = *that which;* *quality of*	audit-or mot-or err-or	*one who* hears. *that which* moves. *quality of* erring.
-ory	adj. *fitted* or = *relating to* n. *place where;* *that which*	preparat-ory armor-y	*fitted* to prepare. *place where* arms are kept.
-ose -ous	= *abounding in*	verb-ose popul-ous	*abounding in* words. *abounding in* people.
-tude	= *condition or* *quality of*	servi-tude forti-tude	*condition of* a slave. *quality of* being brave.
-ty	(See **-ity**.)		
-ule	= *minute*	glob-ule	a *minute* globe.
-ulent	= *abounding in*	op-ulent	*abounding in* wealth.
-ure	= *act or state of;* *that which*	depart-ure creat-ure	*act of* departing. *that which* is created.

(*causing* or *producing*) 1 terror, 2 *sopor-* (sleep), 3 *flor* (a flower), 4 *pestis* (a plague); (*having the quality of*) 5 *farina* (meal), 6 crust, 7 *argilla* (clay), (*becoming*), 8 effervesce.

III.

Write and define verbs denoting to make, render, or perform the act of, from the following words:—

    1 authentic
    2 person
    3 captive
    4 *anima* (life)
    5 *melior* (better)
    6 ample
    7 just
    8 *sanctus* (holy)
    9 pan
    10 false
    11 *facilis* (easy)
    12 *magnus* (great)
    13 equal
    14 fertile
    15 legal

III.—DIRECTIONS IN THE STUDY OF LATIN DERIVATIVES.

1. A **Latin primitive**, or root, is a Latin word from which a certain number of English derivative words is formed. Thus the Latin verb *du'cere*, to draw or lead, is a Latin primitive or root, and from it are formed *educe, education, deduction, ductile, reproductive,* and several hundred other English words.

2. Latin roots consist chiefly of verbs, nouns, and adjectives.

3. English derivatives from Latin words are generally formed not from the root itself but from a part of the root called the *radical*. Thus, in the word "education," the *root-word* is *ducere*, but the *radical* is **duc-** (education = e + **duc** + ate + ion).

4. A **radical** is a word or a part of a word used in forming English derivatives.

5. Sometimes several radicals from the same root-word are used, the different radicals being taken from different grammatical forms of the root-word.

6. Verb-radicals are formed principally from two parts of the verb,—the first person singular of the present indicative, and a part called the *supine*, which is a verbal noun corresponding to the English infinitive in -ing. Thus:—

1st pers. sing. pres. ind.	duco (I draw)
Root	**duc-**
Derivative	*educe*
Supine	ductum (drawing, or to draw)
Root	**duct-**
Derivative	*ductile*

I. In giving a Latin verb-primitive in this book three "principal parts" of the verb will be given, namely: (1) The present infinitive, (2) the first person singular of the present indicative, and (3) the supine—the second and the third parts because from them radicals are obtained, and the infinitive because this is the part used in naming a verb in a general way. Thus as we say that *loved, loving,* etc., are parts of the verb "to love," so we say that *a'mo* (present ind.) and *ama'tum* (supine) are parts of the verb *ama're*.

II. It should be noted that it is incorrect to translate *amo, amatum,* by "to love," since neither of these words is in the infinitive mood, which is *amare*. The indication of the Latin infinitive will be found of great utility, as it is the part by which a Latin verb is referred to in the Dictionary.

7. Noun-radicals and **adjective radicals** are formed from the nominative and from the genitive (or possessive) case of words belonging to these parts of speech. Thus:—

NOM. CASE.	ROOT.	DERIVATIVE.
iter (a journey)	**iter-**.	re*iter*ate

GEN. CASE.	ROOT	DERIVATIVE.
itineris (of a journey)	**itiner-**	*itiner*ant
felicis (nom. *felix*, happy)	**felic-**	*felic*ity

NOTE.—These explanations of the mode of forming radicals are given by way of general information; but this book presupposes and requires no knowledge of Latin, since in every group of English derivatives from Latin, not only the root-words in their several parts, but the *radicals actually used* in word-formation, are given.

Pronunciation of Latin Words.

1. Every word in Latin must have as many syllables as it has vowels or diphthongs: as *miles* (= *mi'les*).

2. *C* is pronounced like *k* before *a, o, u*; and like *s* before *e, i, y*, and the diphthongs *æ* and *œ*: as *cado*, pronounced *ka'do*; *cedo*, pronounced *se'do*.

3. *G* is pronounced hard before *a, o, u*, and soft like *j* before *e, i, y, æ, œ*: as *gusto*, in which *g* is pronounced as in *August*; *gero*, pronounced *je'ro*.

4. A consonant between two vowels must be joined to the latter: as *bene*, pronounced *be'ne*.

5. Two consonants in the middle of a word must be divided: as *mille*, pronounced *mil'le*.

6. The diphthongs *æ* and *œ* are sounded like *e*: as *cædo*, pronounced *ce'do*.

7. Words of two syllables are accented on the first: as *ager*, pronounced *a'jer*.

8. When a word of more than one syllable ends in *a*, the *a* should be sounded like *ah*: as *musa*, pronounced *mu'sah*.

9. *T, s*, and *c*, before *ia, ie, ii, io, iu*, and *eu*, preceded immediately by the accent, in Latin words as in English, change into *sh* and *zh*: as *fa'cio*, pronounced *fa'sheo*; *san'cio*, pronounced *san'sheo*; *spa'tium*, pronounced *spa'sheum*.

NOTE.—According to the Roman method of pronouncing Latin, the vowels *a, e, i, o, u* are pronounced as in *baa, bait, beet, boat, boot*; *ae, au, ei, oe* as in *aisle, our, eight, oil*; *c* always like *k*; *g* as in *get*; *j* as *y* in *yes*; *t* as in *until*; *v* as *w*. See any Latin grammar.

LATIN ROOTS AND ENGLISH DERIVATIVES.

DIVISION I.—METHOD OF STUDY.

1. AG'ERE: a'go, ac'tum, *to do, to drive.*

Radicals: **ag-** and **act-**.

1. **act**, *v.* ANALYSIS: from *actum* by dropping the termination *um*. DEFINITION: to do, to perform. The *noun* "act" is formed in the same way. DEFINITION: a thing done, a deed or performance.

2. **ac'tion**: act + ion = the act of doing: hence, a thing done.

3. **act'ive**: act + ive = having the quality of acting: hence, busy, constantly engaged in action.

4. **act'or**: act + or = one who acts: hence, (1) one who takes part in anything done; (2) a stage player.

5. **a'gent**: ag + ent = one who acts: hence, one who acts or transacts business for another.

6. **ag'ile**: ag + ile = apt to act: hence, nimble, brisk.

7. **co'gent**: from Latin *cogens, cogentis*, pres. part, of *cog'ere* (= *co + agere*, to impel), having the quality of impelling: hence, urgent, forcible.

8. **enact'**: en + act = to put in act: hence, to decree.

9. **transact'**: trans + act = to drive through: hence, to perform.

EXERCISE.

(1.) What two parts of speech is "act"?—Write a sentence containing this word as a verb; another as a noun.—Give a synonym of "act." *Ans. Deed.*—From what is "deed" derived? *Ans.* From the word *do*—hence, literally, something *done*.—Give the distinction between "act" and "deed." *Ans.* "Act" is a *single* action; "deed" is a *voluntary* action: thus—"The *action* which was praised as a good *deed* was but an *act* of necessity."

(2.) Define "action" in oratory; "action" in law.—Combine and define in + action.

(3.) Combine and define in + active; active + ity; in + active + ity.—What is the *negative* of "active"? *Ans. Inactive.*—What is the *contrary* of "active"? *Ans. Passive.*

(4.) Write a sentence containing "actor" in each of its two senses. MODEL: "Washington and Greene were prominent *actors* in the war of the Revolution." "David Garrick, the famous English *actor*, was born in 1716."—What is the feminine of "actor" in the sense of stage player?

(6.) Combine and define agile + ity.—What is the distinction between "active" and "agile"? *Ans.* "Active" implies readiness to act in general; "agile" denotes a readiness to move the *limbs.*—Give two synonyms of "agile." *Ans. Brisk, nimble.* —Give the opposite of "agile." *Ans. Sluggish, inert.*

(7.) Explain what is meant by a "*cogent* argument."—What would be the contrary of a *cogent* argument?

(8.) Combine and define enact + ment.—What is meant by the "*enacting* clause" of a legislative bill?—Write a sentence containing the word "enact." MODEL: "The British Parliament *enacted* the stamp-law in 1765."

(9.) Combine and define transact + ion.—What derivative from "perform" is a synonym of "transaction"?

2. ALIE'NUS, *another, foreign.*

Radical: **alien-**.

1. **al'ien**: from *alienus* by dropping the termination *us*. DEFINITION: a foreigner, one owing allegiance to another country than that in which he is living.

2. **al'ienate**: alien + ate = to cause something to be transferred to another: hence, (1) to transfer title or property to another; (2) to estrange, to withdraw.

3. **inal'ienable**: in + alien + able = that may not be given to another.

EXERCISE.

(1.) Combine and define alien + age.—Can an alien be elected President of the United States? [See the Constitution, Article II. Sec. I. Clause 5.]—What is the word which expresses the process by which a person is changed from an *alien* to a *citizen*?

(2.) Combine and define alienate + ion.—Give a synonym of "alienate" in its *second* sense. *Ans.* To *estrange*.—What is meant by saying that "the oppressive measures of the British government gradually *alienated* the American colonies from the mother country"?

(3.) Quote a passage from the Declaration of Independence containing the word "inalienable."

3. AMA'RE, *to love*, AMI'CUS, *a friend.*

Radicals: **am-** and **amic-**.

1. **a'miable**: am(i) + able = fit to be loved.

> OBS.—The Latin adjective is *amabilis*, from which the English derivative adjective would be *amable*; but it has taken the form am*i*able.

2. **am'ity**: am + ity = the state of being a friend: hence, friendship; good-will.

3. **am'icable**: amic + able = disposed to be a friend: hence, friendly; peaceable.

4. **inim'ical**: through Lat. adj. *inimi'cus*, enemy: hence, inimic(us) + al = inimical, relating to an enemy.

5. **amateur'**: adopted through French *amateur*, from Latin *amator*, a lover: hence, one who cultivates an art from taste or attachment, without pursuing it professionally.

EXERCISE.

(1). What word is a synonym of "amiable"? *Ans. Lovable.*—Show how they are exact synonyms.--Write a sentence containing the word "amiable." MODEL: "The *amiable* qualities of Joseph Warren caused his death to be deeply regretted by all Americans."—What noun can you form from "amiable," meaning the quality of being amiable?—What is the negative of "amiable"? *Ans. Unamiable.*—The contrary? *Ans. Hateful.*

(2.) Give a word that is nearly a synonym of "amity." *Ans. Friendship.*—State the distinction between these words. *Ans.* "Friendship" applies more particularly to individuals; "amity" to societies or nations.—Write a sentence containing the word "amity." MODEL: "The Plymouth colonists in 1621 made a treaty of *amity* with the Indians."—What is the opposite of "amity"?

(3.) Give a synonym of "amicable." *Ans. Friendly.*—Which is the stronger? *Ans. Friendly.*—Why? *Ans.* "Friendly" implies a positive feeling of regard; "amicable" denotes merely the absence of discord.—Write a sentence containing the word "amicable." MODEL: "In 1871 commissioners appointed by the United States and Great Britain made an *amicable* settlement of the Alabama difficulties."

(4.) What is the noun corresponding to the adjective "inimical"? *Ans. Enemy.*— Give its origin. *Ans.* It comes from the Latin *inimicus,* an enemy, through the French *ennemi.*—What preposition does "inimical" take after it? *Ans.* The preposition *to*—thus, "*inimical* to health," "to welfare," etc.

(5.) What is meant by an *amateur* painter? an *amateur* musician?

4. AN'IMUS, *mind, passion*; AN'IMA, *life.*

Radical: **anim-**.

1. **an'imal**: from Lat. n. *anima* through the Latin *animal*: literally, something having life.

2. **animal'cule**: animal + cule = a minute animal: hence, an animal that can be seen only by the microscope.

3. **an'imate**, *v.*: anim + ate = to make alive: hence, to stimulate, or infuse courage.

4. **animos'ity**: anim + ose + ity = the quality of being (ity) full of (ose) passion: hence, violent hatred.

5. **unanim'ity**: un (from *unus*, one) + anim + ity = the state of being of one mind: hence, agreement.

6. **rean'imate**: re + anim + ate = to make alive again: hence, to infuse fresh vigor.

EXERCISE.

(1.) Write a sentence containing the word "animal." MODEL: "Modern science has not yet been able to determine satisfactorily the distinction between an *animal* and a vegetable."

(2.) What is the plural of "animalcule"? *Ans. Animalcules* or *animalculæ.*—Write a sentence containing this word.

(3.) What other part of speech than a verb is "animate"?—What is the negative of the adjective "animate?" *Ans. Inanimate.*—Define it.—Combine and define animate + ion.—Explain what is meant by an "*animated* discussion."

(4.) Give two synonyms of "animosity."

(5.) What is the literal meaning of "unanimity"? If people are of *one mind*, is not this "unanimity"?—What is the adjective corresponding to the noun "unanimity"? —What is the *opposite* of "unanimity"?—Write a sentence containing the word "unanimity."

(6.) Compare the verbs "animate" and "reanimate," and state the signification of each.—Has "reanimate" any other than its literal meaning?—Write a sentence containing this word in its figurative sense. MODEL: "The inspiring words of Lawrence, 'Don't give up the ship!' *reanimated* the courage of the American sailors."—What does "*animated* conversation" mean?

5. AN'NUS, *a year.*

Radical: **ann-**.

1. **an'nals**: from *annus*, through Lat. adj. *annalis*, pertaining to the year: hence, a record of things done from year to year.

2. **an'nual**: through *annuus* (annu + al), relating to a year: hence, yearly or performed in a year.

3. **annu'ity**: through Fr. n. *annuité* = a sum of money payable yearly.

4. **millen'nium**: Lat. n. *millennium* (from *annus* and *mille*, a thousand), a thousand years.

5. **peren'nial**: through Lat. adj. *perennis* (compounded of *per* and *annus*), throughout the year: hence, lasting; perpetual.

EXERCISE.

(1.) Give a synonym of "annals." *Ans. History.*—What is the distinction between "annals" and "history"? *Ans.* "Annals" denotes a mere chronological account of events from year to year; "history," in addition to a narrative of events, inquires into the causes of events.—Write a sentence containing the word "annals," or explain the following sentence: "The *annals* of the Egyptians and Hindoos contain many incredible statements."

(2.) Write a sentence containing the word "annual."

(4.) Write a sentence containing the word "millennium."

(5.) What is the meaning of a "*perennial* plant" in botany? *Ans.* A plant continuing more than two years.—Give the contrary of "perennial." *Ans. Fleeting, short-lived.*

6. ARS, ar'tis, *art, skill.*

Radical: **art-**.

1. **art**: from *artis* by dropping the termination *is*. DEFINITION: 1. cunning—thus, an animal practices *art* in escaping from his pursuers; 2. skill or dexterity—thus, a man may be said to have the *art* of managing his business; 3. a system of rules or a profession—as the *art* of building; 4. creative genius as seen in painting, sculpture, etc., which are called the "fine arts."

2. **art'ist**: art + ist = one who practices an art: hence, a person who occupies himself with one of the fine arts.

> OBS.—A painter is called an artist; but a blacksmith could not properly be so called. The French word *artiste* is sometimes used to denote one who has great skill in some profession, even if it is not one of the fine arts: thus a great genius in cookery might be called an *artiste*.

3. **ar'tisan**: through Fr. n. *artisan,* one who practices an art: hence, one who practices one of the mechanic arts; a workman, or operative.

4. **art'ful**: art + ful = full of art: hence, crafty, cunning.

5. **art'less**: art + less = without art: hence, free from cunning, simple, ingenuous.

6. **ar'tifice**: through Lat. n. *artificium,* something made (*fa'cere,* to make) by art: hence, an artful contrivance or stratagem.

EXERCISE.

(1.) What is the particular meaning of "art" in the sentence from Shakespeare, "There is no *art* to read the mind's construction in the face"?

(2.) Write a sentence containing the word "artist."—Would it be proper to call a famous hair-dresser an *artist*?—What might he be called?—Combine and define artist + ic + al + ly.—What is the negative of "artistic"?

(3.) What is the distinction between an "artist" and an "artisan"?

(5.) Give a synonym of "artless." *Ans. Ingenuous, natural.*—Give the opposite of "artless." *Ans. Wily.*—Combine and define artless + ly; artless + ness.

(6.) Give a synonym of "artifice."—Combine artifice + er.—Does "artificer" mean one who practices artifice?—Write a sentence containing this word.—Combine and define artifice + ial; artifice + al + ity. Give the opposite of "artificial."

7. AUDI'RE: au'dio, audi'tum, *to hear*.

Radicals: **audi-**, and **audit-**.

1. **au'dible**: audi + ble = that may be heard.

2. **au'dience**: audi + ence = literally, the condition of hearing: hence, an assemblage of hearers, an *auditory*.

3. **au'dit**: from *audit(um)* = to hear a statement: hence, to examine accounts.

4. **au'ditor**: audit + or = one who hears, a hearer.

  OBS.—This word has a secondary meaning, namely: an officer who examines accounts.

5. **obe'dient**: through *obediens, obedient(is)*, the present participle of *obedire* (compounded of *ob*, towards, and *audire*): literally, giving ear to: hence, complying with the wishes of another.

EXERCISE.

(1.) "Audible" means that can be heard: what prefix would you affix to it to form a word denoting what can *not* be heard?—What is the adverb from the adjective "audible"?—Write a sentence containing this word.

(2.) What is meant when you read in history of a king's giving *audience*?

(3.) Write a sentence containing the word "audit." MODEL—"The committee which had to *audit* the accounts of Arnold discovered great frauds."—How do you spell the past tense of "audit"?—Why is the *t* not doubled?

(5.) What is the *noun* corresponding to the adjective "obedient"?—What is the *verb* corresponding to these words?—Combine and define dis + obedient.

8. CA'PUT, cap'itis, *the head.*

Radical: **capit-**.

1. **cap'ital,** *a.* and *n.*: capit + al = relating to the *head*: hence, chief, principal, first in importance. DEFINITION: as an adjective it means, (1) principal; (2) great, important; (3) punishable with death;—as a noun it means, (1) the metropolis or seat of government; (2) stock in trade.

2. **capita'tion**: capit + ate + ion = the act of causing heads to be counted: hence, (1) a numbering of persons; (2) a tax upon each head or person.

3. **decap'itate**: de + capit + ate = to cause the head to be taken off; to behead.

4. **prec'ipice**: through Lat. n. *præcipitium*: literally, a headlong descent.

5. **precip'itate**: from Lat. adj. *præcipit(is)*, head foremost. DEFINITION: (1) (*as a verb*) to throw headlong, to press with eagerness, to hasten; (2) (*as an adjective*) headlong, hasty.

EXERCISE.

(1). Write a sentence containing "capital" as an adjective.—Write a sentence containing this word as a noun, in the sense of *city*.—Write a sentence containing "capital" in the sense of *stock*.—Is the *capital* of a state or country necessarily the metropolis or chief city of that state or country?—What is the *capital* of New York state?—What is the *metropolis* of New York State?

(3) Combine and define decapitate + ion.—Can you name an English king who was *decapitated*?—Can you name a French king who was *decapitated*?

(4) What as the meaning of "precipice" in the line, "Swift down the *precipice* of time it goes"?

(5) Combine and define precipitate + ly.—Write a sentence containing the adjective "precipitate". MODEL: "Fabius, the Roman general, is noted for never having made any *precipitate* movements."—Explain the meaning of the verb "precipitate" in the following sentences. "At the battle of Waterloo Wellington *precipitated* the conflict, because he knew Napoleon's army was divided", "The Romans were wont to *precipitate* criminals from the Tarpeian rock."

9. CI'VIS, *a citizen.*

Radical: **civ-**.

1. **civ'ic**: civ + ic = relating to a citizen or to the affairs or honors of a city.

OBS.—The "*civic* crown" in Roman times was a garland of oak-leaves and acorns bestowed on a soldier who had saved the life of a citizen in battle.

2. **civ'il**: Lat adj. *civilis*, meaning (1) belonging to a citizen, (2) of the state, political, (3) polite.

3. **civ'ilize**: civil + ize = to make a savage people into a community having a government, or political organization; hence, to reclaim from a barbarous state.

4. **civiliza'tion**: civil + ize + ate + ion = the state of being civilized.

5. **civil'ian**: civil + (i)an = one whose pursuits are those of civil life—not a soldier.

EXERCISE.

(2.) "What is the ordinary signification of "civil"?—Give a synonym of this word. —Is there any difference between "civil" and "polite"? *Ans.* "Polite" expresses more than "civil," for it is possible to be "civil" without being "polite."—What word would denote the opposite of "civil" in the sense of "polite"?—Combine and define civil + ity.—Do you say *un*civility or *in*civility, to denote the negative of "civility"?—Give a synonym of "uncivil." *Ans. Boorish.*—Give another synonym.

(3.) Write a sentence containing the word "civilize."—Give a participial adjective from this word.—What compound word expresses *half* civilized?—What word denotes a state of society between savage and civilized?

(4.) Give two synonyms of "civilization." *Ans. Culture, refinement.*—What is the meaning of the word "civilization" in the sentence: "The ancient Hindoos and Egyptians had attained a considerable degree of *civilization*"?—Compose a sentence of your own, using this word.

10. COR, cor'dis, *the heart*.

Radical: **cord-**.

1. **core**: from *cor* = the heart: hence, the inner part of a thing.

2. **cor'dial,** *a.*: cord + (i)al = having the quality of the heart: hence, hearty, sincere. The *noun* "cordial" means literally something having the quality of acting on the

heart: hence, a stimulating medicine, and in a figurative sense, something cheering.

3. **con'cord**: con + cord = heart *with (con)* heart: hence, unity of sentiment, harmony.

> OBS.—*Concord* in music is harmony of sound.

4. **dis'cord**: dis + cord = heart *apart from (dis)* heart: hence, disagreement, want of harmony.

5. **record'**: through Lat. v. *recordari,* to remember (literally, to get by *heart*): hence, to register.

6. **cour'age**: through Fr. n. *courage*: literally, *heartiness*: hence, bravery, intrepidity.

> OBS.—The heart is accounted the seat of bravery: hence, the derivative sense of courage.

EXERCISE.

(1.) "The quince was rotten at the *core*"; "The preacher touched the *core* of the subject": in which of these sentences is "core" used in its *literal,* in which in its *figurative,* sense?

(2.) What is the Anglo-Saxon synonym of the adjective "cordial"?—Would you say a "*cordial* laugh" or a "*hearty* laugh"?—What is the opposite of "cordial"?—Combine and define cordial + ly: cordial + ity.— Write a sentence containing the *noun* "cordial" in its figurative sense. MODEL: "Washington's victory at Trenton was like a *cordial* to the flagging spirits of the American army."

(3.) Give a synonym of "concord." *Ans. Accord.*—Supply the proper word: "In your view of this matter, I am in (*accord?* or *concord?*) with you." "There should be —— among friends." "The man who is not moved by —— of sweet sounds."

(4.) What is the connection in meaning between "discord" in music and among brethren?—Give a synonym of this word. *Ans. Strife.*—State the distinction. *Ans.* "Strife" is the stronger: where there is "strife" there must be "discord," but there may be "discord" without "strife"; "discord" consists most in the feeling, "strife" in the outward action.

(5.) What part of speech is "record'"?—When the accent is placed on the first syllable (rec'ord) what part of speech does it become?—Combine and define record + er; un + record + ed.

(6.) "Courage" is the same as having a stout—what?—Give a synonym. *Ans. Fortitude.*—State the distinction. *Ans.* "Courage" enables us to meet danger; "fortitude" gives us strength to endure pain.—Would you say "the Indian shows *courage* when he endures torment without flinching"?—Would you say "The three hundred under Leonidas displayed *fortitude* in opposing the entire Persian army"? —What is the contrary of "courage"?—Combine and define courage + ous; courage + ous + ly.

11. COR'PUS, cor'poris, *the body*.

Radical: **corpor-**.

1. **cor'poral**: corpor + al = relating to the *body*.

> OBS.—The noun "corporal," meaning a petty officer, is not derived from *corpus*: it comes from the French *caporal*, of which it is a corruption.

2. **cor'porate**: corpor + ate = made into a body: hence, united into a body or corporation.

3. **incor'porate**: in + corpor + ate = to make into a body: hence, (1) to form into a legal body; (2) to unite one substance with another.

4. **corpora'tion**: corpor + ate + ion = that which is made into a body: hence, a body politic, authorized by law to act as one person.

5. **cor'pulent**: through Lat. adj. *corpulentus*, fleshy: hence, stout in body, fleshy.

6. **cor'puscle**: corpus + cle = a diminutive body; hence, a minute particle of matter.

7. **corps**: [pronounced *core*] through Fr. n. *corps*, a body. DEFINITION: (1) a body of troops; (2) a body of individuals engaged in some one profession.

8. **corpse**: through Fr. n. *corps*, the body; that is, *only* the body—the spirit being departed: hence, the dead body of a human being.

EXERCISE.

(1.) Give two synonyms of "corporal." *Ans. Corporeal* and *bodily*.—What is the distinction between "corporal" and "corporeal"? *Ans.* "Corporal" means pertaining to the body; "corporeal" signifies material, as opposed to spiritual.—Would you say a *corporal* or a *corporeal* substance? *corporal* or *corporeal* punishment? Would you say *corporal* strength or *bodily* strength?

(3.) Write a sentence containing the verb "incorporate" in its *first* sense. MODEL: "The London company which settled Virginia was *incorporated* in 1606, and received a charter from King James I."

(4.) Write a sentence containing the word "corporation." [Find out by what corporation Massachusetts Bay Colony was settled, and write a sentence about that.]

(5.) What noun is there corresponding to the adjective "corpulent" and synonymous with "stoutness"?—Give two synonyms of "corpulent." *Ans. Stout, lusty.*—What is the distinction? *Ans.* "Corpulent" means fat; "stout" and "lusty" denote a strong frame.

(6.) What is meant by an "army *corps*"? *Ans.* A body of from twenty to forty thousand soldiers, forming several brigades and divisions.

(7.) How is the plural of corps spelled? *Ans. Corps.* How pronounced? *Ans. Cores.* —What is meant by the "diplomatic *corps*"?

(8.) What other form of the word "corpse" is used? *Ans.* The form *corse* is sometimes used in poetry; as in the poem on the Burial of Sir John Moore:

> "Not a drum was heard, not a funeral note,
> As his *corse* to the ramparts we hurried."

12. CRED'ERE: cre'do, cred'itum, *to believe.*

Radicals: **cred-** and **credit-**.

1. **creed**: from the word *credo,* "I believe," at the beginning of the Apostles' Creed: hence, a summary of Christian belief.

2. **cred'ible**: cred + ible = that may be believed: hence, worthy of belief.

3. **cred'it**: from credit(um) = belief, trust: hence, (1) faith; (2) reputation; (3) trust given or received.

4. **cred'ulous**: through the Lat. adj. *credulus,* easy of belief: credul + ous = abounding in belief: hence, believing easily.

5. **discred'it**: dis + credit = to *dis*believe.

EXERCISE.

(2.) Write a sentence containing the word "credible." MODEL: "When the King of Siam was told that in Europe the water at certain seasons could be walked on, he declared that the statement was not *credible*."—What single word will express *not credible*?—Combine and define credible + ity.—Give a synonym of "credible." *Ans. Trustworthy.*—State the distinction. *Ans.* "Credible" is generally applied to things, as "*credible* testimony"; "trustworthy" to persons, as "a *trustworthy* witness."

(3.) What is the meaning of *credit* in the passage,

"John Gilpin was a citizen
Of *credit* and renown"?

Give a synonym of this word. *Ans. Trust.*—What is the distinction? *Ans.* "Trust" looks forward; "credit" looks back—we *credit* what has happened; we *trust* what is to happen.—What other part of speech than a noun is "credit"?—Combine and define credit + ed.—Why is the *t* not doubled?

(4.) What is the meaning of "credulous" in the passage,

"So glistened the dire snake, and into fraud
Led Eve, our *credulous* mother"?—MILTON.

What noun corresponding to the adjective "credulous" will express the quality of believing too easily?—What is the negative of "credulous"?— What is the distinction between "incredible" and "incredulous"?—Which applies to persons? which to things?

(5.) To what two parts of speech does "discredit" belong?—Write a sentence containing this word as a *noun*; another as a *verb*.

13. CUR'RERE: cur'ro, cur'sum, *to run.*

Radicals used: **curr-** and **curs-**.

1. **cur'rent**, *a.*: curr + ent = running: hence, (1) passing from person to person, as a "*current* report"; (2) now in progress, as the "*current* month."

2. **cur'rency**: curr + ency = the state of passing from person to person, as "the report obtained *currency*": hence circulation.

   OBS.—As applied to money, it means that it is in circulation or passing from hand to hand, as a representative of value.

3. **cur'sory**: curs + ory = runn*ing* or pass*ing*: hence, hasty.

4. **excur'sion**: ex + curs + ion = the act of running out: hence, an expedition or jaunt.

5. **incur'sion**: in + curs + ion = the act of running in: hence, an invasion.

6. **precur'sor**: pre + curs + or = one who runs before: hence a forerunner.

EXERCISE.

(1.) What other part of speech than an adjective is "current"?—What is now the *current* year?

(2.) Why are there two r's in "currency"? *Ans.* Because there are two in the root *currere.*—Give a synonym of this word in the sense of "money." *Ans.* The "circulating medium."—What was the "currency" of the Indians in early times?—Compose a sentence using this word.

(3.) When a speaker says that he will cast a "*cursory* glance" at a subject, what does he mean?—Combine and define cursory + ly.

(4.) Is "excursion" usually employed to denote an expedition in a friendly or a hostile sense?

(5.) Is "incursion" usually employed to denote an expedition in a friendly or a hostile sense?—Give a synonym. *Ans. Invasion.*—Which implies a hasty expedition?—Compose a sentence containing the word *incursion*. MODEL: "The Parthians were long famed for their rapid *incursions* into the territory of their enemies."

(6.) What is meant by saying that John the Baptist was the *precursor* of Christ?—What is meant by saying that black clouds are the *precursor* of a storm?

14. DIG'NUS, *worthy.*

Radical: **dign-**.

1. **dig'nify**: dign + (*i*)fy = to make of worth: hence, to advance to honor.

2. **dig'nity**: dign + ity = the state of being of worth: hence, behavior fitted to inspire respect.

3. **indig'nity**: in + dign + ity = the act of treating a person in an unworthy (*indignus*) manner: hence, insult, contumely.

4. **condign'**: con + dign = very worthy: hence, merited, deserved.

OBS.—The prefix *con* is here merely intensive.

EXERCISE.

(1.) What participial adjective is formed from the verb "dignify"? *Ans. Dignified.*—Give a stronger word. *Ans. Majestic.*—Give a word which denotes the same thing carried to excess and becoming ridiculous. *Ans. Pompous.*

(2.) Can you mention a character in American history remarkable for the dignity of his behavior?—Compose a sentence containing this word.

(3.) Give the plural of "indignity."—What is meant by saying that "indignities were heaped on" a person?

(4.) How is the word "condign" now most frequently employed? *Ans.* In connection with punishment: thus we speak of "*condign* punishment," meaning richly deserved punishment.

15. DOCE'RE: do'ceo, doc'tum, *to teach.*

Radicals: **doc-** and **doct-**.

1. **doc'ile**: doc + ile = that may be taught: hence, teachable.

2. **doc'tor**: doct + or = one who teaches: hence, one who has taken the highest degree in a university authorizing him to practice and teach.

4. **doc'trine**: through Lat. n. *doctrina,* something taught; hence, a principle taught as part of a system of belief.

EXERCISE.

(1.) Combine and define docile + ity.—Give the opposite of "docile." *Ans. Indocile.*—Mention an animal that is very docile.—Mention one remarkable for its want of docility.

(2.) What is meant by "*Doctor* of Medicine"?—Give the abbreviation.—What does LL.D. mean? *Ans.* It stands for the words *legum doctor*, doctor of laws: the double L marks the plural of the Latin noun.

(3.) Give two synonyms of "doctrine." *Ans. Precept, tenet.*—What does "tenet" literally mean? *Ans.* Something *held*—from Lat. v. *tenere*, to hold.—Combine and define doctrine + al.

16. DOM'INUS, *a master or lord.*

Radical: **domin-**.

1. **domin'ion**: domin + ion = the act of exercising mastery: hence, (1) rule; (2) a territory ruled over.

2. **dom'inant**: domin + ant = relating to lordship or mastery: hence, prevailing.

3. **domineer'**: through Fr. v. *dominer*; literally, to "*lord* it" over one: hence, to rule with insolence.

4. **predom'inate**: pre + domin + ate = to cause one to be master *before* another: hence, to be superior, to rule.

EXERCISE.

(1.) What is meant by saying that "in 1776 the United Colonies threw off the *dominion* of Great Britain"?

(2.) What is meant by the "*dominant* party"? a "*dominant* race"?

(3.) Compose a sentence containing the word "domineer." MODEL: "The blustering tyrant, Sir Edmund Andros, *domineered* for several years over the New England colonies; but his misrule came to an end in 1688 with the accession of King William."

(4.) "The Republicans at present *predominate* in Mexico": what does this mean?

17. FI'NIS, *an end or limit.*

Radical: **fin-**.

1. **fi'nite**: fin + ite = having the quality of coming to an end: hence, limited in quantity or degree.

2. **fin'ish**: through Fr. v. *finir*; literally, to bring to an end: hence, to complete.

3. **infin'ity**: in + fin + ity = the state of having no limit: hence, unlimited extent of time, space, or quantity.

4. **define'**: through Fr. v. *definer*; literally, to bring a thing down to its limits: hence, to determine with precision.

5. **confine'**: con + fine; literally, to bring within limits or bounds: hence, to restrain.

6. **affin'ity**: af (a form of prefix *ad*) + fin + ity = close agreement.

EXERCISE.

(1.) What is meant by saying that "the human faculties are *finite*"?

(2.) What is the opposite of "finite"?—Give a synonym. *Ans. Limited.*—What participial adjective is formed from the verb to "finish"?—What is meant by a "*finished* gentleman"?

(3.) Give a synonym of "infinity." *Ans. Boundlessness.*—"The microscope reveals the fact that each drop of water contains an *infinity* of animalculæ." What is the sense of *infinity* as used in this sentence?

(4.) Combine define + ite; in + define + ite.—Analyze the word "definition."—Compose a sentence containing the word "define."

(5.) Combine and define confine + ment.—What other part of speech than a verb is "confine"? *Ans.* A noun.—Write a sentence containing the word "confines."

(6.) Find in the dictionary the meaning of "chemical *affinity*."

18. FLU'ERE: flu'o, flux'um, *to flow.*

Radicals: **flu-** and **flux-**.

1. **flux**: from flux*um* = a flowing.

2. **flu'ent**: flu + ent = having the quality of flowing. Used in reference to language it means *flowing* speech: hence, voluble.

3. **flu'id,** *n.*: flu + id = Flow*ing*: hence, anything that flows.

4. **flu'ency**: flu + ency = state of flowing (in reference to language).

5. **af'fluence**: af (form of *ad*) + flu + ence = a flowing *to*: hence, an abundant supply, as of thought, words, money, etc.

6. **con'fluence**: con + flu + ence = a flowing together: hence, (1) the flowing together of two or more streams; (2) an assemblage, a union.

7. **in'flux**: in + flux = a flowing in or into.

8. **super'fluous**: super + flu + ous = having the quality of *over*flowing: hence, needless, excessive.

EXERCISE.

(2.) What is meant by a "fluent" speaker?—What word would denote a speaker who is the reverse of "fluent"?

(3.) Write a sentence containing the word "fluid."

(4.) What is meant by "fluency" of style?

(5.) What is the ordinary use of the word "affluence"? An "*affluence* of ideas," means what?

(6.) Compose a sentence containing the word "confluence." MODEL: "New York City stands at the —— of two streams."

(8.) Mention a noun corresponding to the adjective "superfluous."—Compose a sentence containing the word "superfluous."—What is its opposite? *Ans. Scanty, meager.*

19. GREX, gre'gis, *a flock or herd.*

Radical: **greg-**.

1. **ag'gregate**, *v.*: ag (for *ad*) + greg + ate = to cause to be brought into a flock: hence, to gather, to assemble.

2. **egre'gious**: e + greg + (i)ous, through Lat. adj. *egre'gius*, chosen from the herd: hence, remarkable.

OBS.—Its present use is in association with inferiority.

3. **con'gregate**: con + greg + ate = to perform the act of flocking together: hence, to assemble.

EXERCISE.

(1.) What other part of speech than a verb is "aggregate"?—Why is this word spelled with a double *g*?

(2.) Combine and define egregious + ly.—What does an "*egregious* blunder" mean?—Compose a sentence containing the word "egregious."

(3.) Why is it incorrect to speak of congregating *together*?—Combine and define congregate + ion.

20. I'RE: e'o, i'tum, *to go.*

Radical: **it-**.

1. **ambi'tion**: amb (around) + it + ion = the act of going around. DEFINITION: an eager desire for superiority or power.

OBS.—This meaning arose from the habit of candidates for office in Rome *going around* to solicit votes: hence, aspiration for office, and finally, aspiration in general.

2. **ini'tial**, *a.*: in + it + (i)al = pertaining to the *in*going: hence, marking the commencement.

3. **ini'tiate**: in + it + (i)ate = to cause one to go in: hence, to introduce, to commence.

4. **sedi'tion**: sed (*aside*) + it + ion = the act of going *aside*; that is, going to a separate and insurrectionary party.

5. **trans'it**: trans + it = a passing across: hence, (1) the act of passing; (2) the line of passage; (3) a term in astronomy.

6. **tran'sitory**: trans + it + ory = pass*ing* over: hence, brief, fleeting.

EXERCISE.

(1.) Compose a sentence containing the word "ambition." MODEL: "Napoleon's *ambition* was his own greatness; Washington's, the greatness of his country."—What is meant by "military ambition"? "political ambition"? "literary ambition"?—What adjective means *possessing ambition*?—Combine and define un + ambitious.

(2.) What is the opposite of "initial"? *Ans. Final, closing.*—What part of speech is "initial" besides an adjective?—What is meant by "initials"?

(3.) What is meant by saying that "the campaign of 1775 was *initiated* by an attack on the British in Boston"?—Give the opposite of "initiate" in the sense of "commence."

(4.) Give a synonym of "sedition." *Ans. Insurrection.*—Give another.—Compose a sentence containing this word.

(5.) Explain what is meant by goods "in *transit*."—Explain what is meant by the "Nicaragua *transit*."—When you speak of the *transit* of Venus," you are using a term in what science?

(6.) Give a synonym of "transitory."—Give its opposite. *Ans. Permanent, abiding.*

21. LA'PIS, lap'idis, *a stone.*

1. **lap'idary**: lapid + ary = one who works in stone: hence, one who cuts, polishes, and engraves precious stones.

2. **dilap'idated**: di + lapid + ate + ed = put into the condition of a building in which the stones are falling apart: hence, fallen into ruin, decayed.

3. **dilapida'tion**: di + lapid + ate + ion = the state (of a building) in which the stones are falling apart: hence, demolition, decay.

EXERCISE.

Use the word "lapidary" in a sentence. MODEL: "When Queen Victoria wanted the Koh-i-noor to be recut, she sent it to a famous *lapidary* in Holland."

(2.) Write a sentence containing the word "dilapidated." MODEL: "At Newport, Rhode Island, there stands a *dilapidated* mill, which some writers have foolishly believed to be a tower built by Norsemen in the twelfth century."—If we should speak of a "*dilapidated* fortune," would the word be used in its literal meaning or in a figurative sense?

(3.) Give two synonyms of "dilapidation." *Ans. Ruin, decay.*

22. LEX, le'gis, *a law or rule*.

Radical: **leg-**.

1. **le'gal**: leg + al = relating to the law; lawful.

2. **ille'gal**: il (for *in*, not) + leg + al = not legal: hence, unlawful.

3. **leg'islate**: from *legis* + *latum* (from Lat. v. *fer're*, *latum*, to bring), to bring forward: hence, to make or pass laws.

4. **legit'imate**: through Lat. adj. *legitimus*, lawful; legitim (us) + ate = made lawful: hence, in accordance with established law.

5. **priv'ilege**: Lat. adj. *privus*, private; literally, a law passed for the benefit of a private individual: hence, a franchise, prerogative, or right.

EXERCISE.

(1.) Point out the different senses of "legal" in the two expressions, "the *legal* profession" and "a *legal* right."—Combine and define legal + ize.

(2.) Give an Anglo-Saxon synonym of "illegal." *Ans. Unlawful.*—Show that they are synonyms. *Ans.* il (*in*) = un; *leg* = law; and al = ful.—Compose a sentence containing the word "illegal."—Combine and define illegal + ity.

(3.) What noun derived from "legislate" means the law-making power?—Combine and define legislate + ion; legislate + ive.

(4.) Give the negative of "legitimate."

(5.) What is the plural of "privilege"?—Define the meaning of this word in the passage,—

> "He claims his *privilege*, and says 't is fit
> Nothing should be the judge of wit, but wit."

23. LIT'ERA, *a letter*.

Radical: **liter-**.

1. **lit'eral**: liter + al = relating to the letter of a thing; that is, exact to the letter.

2. **lit'erary**: liter + ary = pertaining to *letters* or learning.

3. **obliterate**: ob + liter + ate = to cause letters to be rubbed out: hence, to rub out, in general.

4. **lit'erature**: through Lat. n. *literatura* = the collective body of literary works.

5. **illit'erate**: il (for *in*, not) + liter + ate = of the nature of one who does not know his letters.

(1.) Define what is meant by a "*literal* translation."

(2.) Give a synonymous expression for a "literary man."—Compose a sentence containing the terms "literary society."

(3.) Give a synonym of "obliterate" in its literal meaning. *Ans.* To *erase.*—If we should speak of *obliterating* the memory of a wrong, would the word be used in its primary or its derivative sense?

(4.) "When we speak of English "literature" what is meant?—Can you mention a great poem in Greek "literature"?—Compose a sentence containing the word "literature."

(5.) Give a synonym of "illiterate." *Ans. Unlearned.*—What is the opposite of "illiterate"? *Ans. Learned.*

24. MORS, mortis, *death.*

Radical: **mort-.**

1. **mor'tal**: mort + a = relating to death.

2. **mor'tify**: mort + ify = literally, to cause to die: hence, (1) to destroy vital functions; (2) to humble.

3. **immor'talize**: im (for *in,* not) + mort + al + ize = to make not subject to death: hence, to perpetuate.

EXERCISE.

(1.) What does Shakespeare mean by the expression to "shuffle off this *mortal* coil"?—Combine and define mortal + ity.—What is the opposite of "mortal"?—Give a synonym. *Ans. Deathless.*

(2.) State the two meanings of "mortify."—What noun is derived from this verb? *Ans. Mortification.*—When a surgeon speaks of "mortification" setting in, what does he mean?—What is meant by "mortification" when we say that the British felt great *mortification* at the recapture of Stony Point by General Anthony Wayne?

(3.) Compose a sentence containing the word "immortalize." MODEL: "Milton *immortalized* his name by the production of Paradise Lost."

25. NOR'MA, *a rule.*

Radical: **norm-**.

1. **nor'mal**: norm + al = according to rule.

2. **enor'mous**: e + norm + ous = having the quality of being out of all rule: hence, excessive, huge.

3. **enor'mity**: e + norm + ity = the state of being out of all rule: hence, an excessive degree—generally used in regard to bad qualities.

4. **abnor'mal**: ab + norm + al = having the quality of being *away* from the usual rule: hence, unnatural.

EXERCISE.

(1.) What is meant by the expression, "the *normal* condition of things"? —"What is the meaning of the term a "*normal* school"? *Ans.* It means a school whose methods of instruction are to serve as a model for imitation; a school for the education of teachers.

(2.) Give a synonym of "enormous." *Ans. Immense.*—Give another. —"What is meant by "*enormous* strength"? an "*enormous* crime?"— Combine and define enormous + ly.

(3.) Illustrate the meaning of the word "enormity" by a sentence.

26. OR'DO, or'dinis, *order.*

Radical: **ordin-**.

1. **or'dinary**: ordin + ary = relating to the usual order of things.

2. **extraor'dinary**: extra + ordin + ary = beyond ordinary.

3. **inor'dinate**: in + ordin + ate = having the quality of not being within the usual order of things: hence, excessive.

4. **subor'dinate**: sub + ordin + ate = having the quality of being under the usual order: hence, inferior, secondary.

5. **or'dinance**: ordin + ance = that which is according to order: hence, a law.

6. **insubordina'tion**: in + sub + ordin + ate + ion = the state of not being under the usual order of things: hence, disobedience to lawful authority.

EXERCISE.

(1.) What is meant by "*ordinary* language"? an "*ordinary* man"?

(2.) Combine and define extraordinary + ly.—Compose a sentence using the word "extraordinary."—Give a synonym of "extraordinary." *Ans. Unusual.*

(3.) Explain what is meant by saying that General Charles Lee had "*inordinate* vanity."—Is "inordinate" used with reference to praiseworthy things?

(4.) What part of speech other than an adjective is "subordinate"?—What is meant by "a *subordinate*"?—What does "subordinate" mean in the sentence, "We must *subordinate* our wishes to the rules of morality"?—Combine and define subordinate + ion.

(5.) What does the expression "the *ordinances* of the Common Council of the City of New York" mean?

(6.) Compose a sentence containing the word "insubordination."—Give the opposite of "insubordination"? *Ans. Subordination, obedience.*

27. PARS, par'tis, *a part or share.*

Radical: **part-**.

1. **part**: from part*is* = a share.

2. **par'ticle**: part + (*i*)cle = a small part.

3. **par'tial**: part + (*i*)al = relating to a part rather than the whole: hence, inclined to favor one party or person or thing.

4. **par'ty**: through Fr. n. *partie:* a set of persons (that is, a part of the people) engaged in some design.

5. **par'tisan**: through Fr. n. *partisan* = a party man.

6. **depart'**: de + part = to take one's self away from one part to another.

EXERCISE.

(1.) What part of speech is "part" besides a noun?—Write a sentence containing this word as a noun; another as a verb.

(2.) Point out the connection of meaning between "particle" and "particular." *Ans.* "Particular'" means taking note of the minute parts or *particles* of a given subject.

(3.) What is the negative of "partial"? *Ans. Impartial.*—Define it.

(4.) Explain what is meant by a "political *party.*"

(6.) Combine and define depart + ure.

28. PES, pe'dis, *a foot.*

Radical: **ped-**.

1. **ped'al**: ped + al = an instrument made to be moved by the foot.

2. **bi'ped**: bi + ped = a two-footed animal.

3. **quad'ruped**: quadru + ped = a four-footed animal. (*Quadru*, from *quatuor*, four.)

4. **ped'dler**: literally, a trader who travels on foot.

5. **expedite'**: ex + ped + ite (*ite*, equivalent to *ate*) = literally, to free the feet from entanglement: hence, to hasten.

6. **expedi'tion**: ex + ped + ite + ion = the act of expediting: hence, (1) the quality of being expeditious, promptness; (2) a sending forth for the execution of some object of importance.

7. **imped'iment**: through Lat. n. *impedimentum*; literally, something which *impedes* or entangles the feet: hence, an obstacle, an obstruction.

EXERCISE.

(2.) Make up a sentence containing the word "biped."

(3.) Make up a sentence containing the word "quadruped."

(4.) What is the English verb from which "peddler" comes?—In what other way is "peddler" sometimes spelled? *Ans.* It is sometimes spelled with but one *d*—thus, *pedler*.

(5.) "To expedite the growth of plants": what does that mean?—Give the opposite of "expedite." *Ans.* To *retard*.

(6.) Point out the double sense of the word "expedition" in the following sentences: "With winged *expedition*, swift as lightning."—*Milton*. "The *expedition* of Cortez miserably failed."—*Prescott*.

(7.) Compose a sentence containing the word "impediment."—What is meant by "*impediment* of speech"?—Is the word here used in its literal or its figurative sense?

29. RUM'PERE: rum'po, rup'tum, *to break.*

Radical: **rupt-**.

1. **rup'ture**: rupt + ure = the act of breaking with another; that is, a *breach* of friendly relations.

2. **erup'tion**: e + rupt + ion = the act of breaking or bursting out.

3. **abrupt'**: ab + rupt = broken off short: hence, having a sudden termination.

4. **corrupt'**: cor (for *con*) + rupt = thoroughly broken up: hence, decomposed, depraved.

5. **interrupt'**: inter + rupt = to break in between: hence, to hinder.

6. **bank'rupt**: literally, one who is bank-broken, who cannot pay his debts, an insolvent debtor.

EXERCISE.

(1.) What other part of speech than a noun is "rupture"? *Ans*. A verb.— Compose one sentence using the word as a verb, the other as a noun.— What does the "*rupture* of a blood vessel" mean? Is this the literal sense of the word?—The "*rupture* of friendly relations" between Maine and Massachusetts: is this its literal or its figurative sense?

(2.) Compose a sentence containing the word "eruption."

(3.) Combine and define abrupt + ness; abrupt + ly.—When we speak of an "*abrupt* manner," what is meant?—When we speak of an "*abrupt* descent," what is meant?

(4.) Explain what is meant by "corrupt principles"; a "*corrupt* judge."— Combine and define corrupt + ion; corrupt + ible; in + corrupt + ible.— What other part of speech than an adjective is "corrupt"?—What part of speech is it in the sentence "evil communications *corrupt* good manners"?

30. TEM'PUS, tem'poris, *time*.

Radical: **tempor-**.

1. **tem'poral**: tempor + al = relating to time: hence, not everlasting.

2. **tem'porary**: tempor + ary = lasting only for a brief time.

3. **contem'porary**: con + tempor + ary = one who lives in the same time with another.

4. **tem'perance**: through Fr. n. *tempérance*; literal meaning, the state of being *well timed* as to one's habits: hence, moderation.

5. **extempora'neous**: ex + temporane(us) + ous = produced at the time.

6. **tem'porize**: tempor + ize = to do as the times do: hence, to yield to the current of opinion.

EXERCISE.

(1.) Give the opposite of "temporal." *Ans. Eternal.* Illustrate these two words by a sentence from the Bible. *Ans.* "The things which are seen are *temporal*; but the things which are not seen are *eternal.*"

(2.) Give the opposite of "temporary." *Ans. Permanent.*—What is meant by the "*temporary* government of a city"?—Give a synonym of "temporary." *Ans. Transitory.*—Would you say that man is a "*temporary* being" or a "*transitory* being"?

(3.) Compose a sentence illustrating the use of the word "contemporary."—What adjective corresponds to this adjective?

(4.) State the distinction between "temperance" and "abstinence."—Write a sentence showing the use of the two words.

(5.) What is meant by an "*extemporaneous* speech?"

(6.) What is one who *temporizes* sometimes called? *Ans.* A *time*-server.

DIVISION II.—ABBREVIATED LATIN DERIVATIVES.

NOTE—In Division II, the English derivatives from Latin roots are given in abbreviated form, and are arranged in paragraphs under the particular *radicals*, from which the several groups of derivatives are formed. The radicals are printed at the left in bold-face type—thus., **acr-, acerb-,** etc. Derivatives not obviously connected with the Latin roots are given in the last paragraph of each section. Pupils are required to unite the prefixes and suffixes with the radicals, thus forming the English derivatives, which may be given either orally or in writing. Only difficult definitions are appended: in the case of words not defined, pupils may be required to form the definition by reference to the signification of the radicals and the formative elements, thus, acr + id = acrid, being bitter, acr + id + ity = state of being bitter, bitterness.

1. A'CER, a'cris, sharp; Acer'bus, bitter; Ac'idus, sour; Ace'tum, vinegar.

acr: -id, -idity; ac'rimony (Lat. n. *acrimo'nia*, sharpness of temper); acrimo'nious.

acerb: -ity; exac'erbate, *to render bitter;* exacerba'tion.

acid: ac'id; -ify, -ity; acid'ulate (Lat. adj. *acid'ulus*, slightly sour); acid'ulous; subac'id, *slightly acid.*

acet: -ate, *a certain salt;* -ic, *pertaining to a certain acid;* -ify, -ification, -ose, -ous.

2. AE'DES, a house.

ed: ed'ify; edifica'tion; ed'ifice (Lat. n. *edifi'cium*, a large building); e'dile (Lat. n. *aedi'lis*, a Roman magistrate who had charge of buildings).

3. Æ'QUUS, equal: Æqua'lis, equal, just.

equ: -able, -ation, -ator, -atorial, -ity, -itable; ad'equate (Lat. v. *adequa're*, *adequa'tum*, to make equal); inadequacy; inad'equate; iniq'uity (Lat. n. *iniq'uitas*, want of equal or just dealing); iniq'uitous.

equal: e'qual (n., v., adj.), -ity, -ize; co-e'qual; une'qual.

4. Æ'VUM, an age; Æter'nitas, eternal.

ev: co-e'val; longevity (Lat. adj. *lon'gus*, long); prime'val (Lat. adj. *pri'mus*, first).

etern: -al, -ity, -ize; co-eter'nal.

5. A'GER, a'gri, a field, land.

agri: agra'rian (Lat. adj. *agrarius*, relating to land); agra'rianism; ag'riculture (Lat. n. *cultu'ra*, cultivation), agricult'ural, agricult'urist.

Per'egrinate (Lat. v. *peregrina'ri*, to travel in foreign lands); peregrina'tion; pil'grim (Fr. n. *pélérin*, a wanderer); pil'grimage.

AGERE, to do. (See p. 23.)

6. AL'ERE: a'lo, al'itum or al'tum, to nourish; ALES'CERE: ales'co to grow up.

al: al'iment (Lat. n. *alimen'tum,* nourishment); alimen'tary; al'imony (Lat. n. *alimo'ma,* allowance made to a divorced wife for her support).

alit: coali'tion (-ist).

alesc: coalesce' (-ence, -ent).

ALIENUS. (See p. 25.)

7. AL'TER, another; Alter'nus, one after another.

alter: al'ter, -ation, -ative (a medicine producing a change); unal'tered; alterca'tion (Lat. n. *alterca'tio,* a contention).

altern: -ate, -ation, -ative; subal'tern, *a subordinate officer.*

AMARE; Amicus. (See p. 25.)

ANIMUS; Anima. (See p. 26.)

ANNUS. (See p. 27.)

8. ANTI'QUUS, old, ancient.

antiqu: -ary, -arian, -ated, -ity; antique' (Fr. adj. *antique*), *old, ancient.*

9. AP'TUS, fit, suitable.

apt: apt, -itude, -ly, -ness; adapt' (-able, -ation, -or).

10. A'QUA, water.

aque: -duct (*du'cere*, to lead); a'queous; suba'queous; terra'queous (Lat. n. *terra*, land); aquat'ic (Lat. adj. *aquat'icus*, relating to water); aqua'rium (Lat. n. *aqua'rium*, a reservoir of water), *a tank for water-plants and animals.*

11. AR'BITER, ar'bitri, a judge or umpire.

arbiter: ar'biter, *a judge or umpire.*

arbitr: -ary, -ate, -ation, -ator; arbit'rament (Lat. n. *arbitramen'tum*, decision).

12. AR'BOR, ar'boris, a tree.

arbor: ar'bor, *a lattice-work covered with vines, etc., a bower*; -et, *a little tree*; -ist, -escent, -(e)ous; arbore'tum, *a place where specimens of trees are cultivated*; arboricult'ure (-ist).

13. AR'MA, arms, weapons.

arm: arm (n. and v.); arms, *weapons*; -or, *defensive weapons*; ar'morer; ar'mory; armo'rial, *belonging to the escutcheon or coat of arms of a family*; ar'mistice (*sis'tere*, to cause to stand still); disarm'; unarmed'.

Arma'da (Span, n.), *a naval warlike force*; ar'my (Fr. n *armée*); ar'mament (Lat. n. *armamen'ta*, utensils); armadil'lo (Span, n.), *an animal armed with a bony shell.*

ARS. (See page 28.)

14. ARTIC'ULUS, a little joint.

articul: -ate (v., to utter in distinctly *jointed* syllables), -ate (adj. formed with joints), -ation; inartic'ulate; ar'ticle (Fr. n. *article*).

15. AS'PER, rough.

asper: -ate, -ity; exas'perate; exas'peration.

AUDIRE. (See page 29.)

16. AUGE'RE: au'geo, auc'tum, to increase.

aug: augment' (v.); augmentation.

auct: -ion, *a sale in which the price is increased by bidders*; -ioneer. Author (Lat. n. *auc'tor*, one who increases knowledge); author'ity; au'thorize; auxil'iary (Lat. n. *auxil'ium*, help).

17. A'VIS, a bird; Au'gur, Aus'pex, aus'picis, a soothsayer.

augur: au'gur (n.), *one who foretells future events by observing the flight of birds*, (v.) *to foretell*; au'gury, *an omen*; inau'gurate, *to invest with an office by solemn rites*; inaugura'tion; inau'gural.

auspici: -ous, *favorable*; inauspi'cious; aus'pices.

18. BAR'BARUS, savage, uncivilized.

barbar: -ian (n. and adj.), -ic, -ism, -ity, -ize, -ous.

19. BIS, twice or two.

bi: bi'ennial (Lat. n. *an'nus*, a year); big'amy (Greek n. *gamos*, marriage); bil'lion (Lat. n. *mil'lio*, a million; literally, twice a million); bipar'tite (Lat. n. *pars, par'tis*, a part); bi'ped (Lat. n. *pes, pe'dis*, foot); bis'cuit (Fr. v. *cuit*, cooked); bisect' (Lat. v. *sec'tum*, cut); bi'valve (Lat. n. *val'væ*, folding-doors); bi'nary (Lat. adj. *bi'ni*, two by two); binoc'ular (Lat. n. *oc'ulus*, the eye); combine'; combina'tion.

20. BO'NIS, good; Be'ne, well.

bonus: bonus (something to the *good* of a person in addition to compensation), bounty (Fr. n. *bonté*, kindness); boun'teous; boun'tiful.

bene: ben'efice (Lat. v. *fac'ere, fac'tum,* to do), literally, *a benefit, an ecclesiastical living;* benef'icence; benef'icent; benefi'cial; ben'efit; benefac'tion; benefac'tor; benedic'tion (Lat. v. *dic'ere, dic'tum,* to say); benev'olence (Lat. v. *vel'le,* to will).

EXERCISE.

In this and the following exercises, tell the roots of the words printed in italic: The *equator* divides the globe into two *equal* parts. Good *agriculturists* read *agricultural* papers. In the *primeval* ages the *longevity* of man was very great. The *pilgrims* have gone on a *pilgrimage* to the Holy Land. The *subaltern* had no *alternative* but to obey. To remove the stain a powerful *acid* must be used. The *alimony* which had hitherto been allowed was no longer considered *adequate.* The discourse, though learned, was not *edifying.* God is an *eternal* and unchangeable being. The handsome *edifice* was burned to the ground. The plants and animals in the *aquarium* were brought from abroad. Though the style is *antiquated,* it is not inelegant. The *arbitrary* proceedings of the British Parliament *exasperated* the Americans. God is the *bountiful* Giver of all good. The President made a short *inaugural* address. By *combined* effort success is sure. One of Scott's novels is called The *Antiquary.* It is *barbarous* needlessly to destroy life. George Peabody was noted for his *benevolence.* The Romans were famous for their great *aqueducts.*

21. CAD'ERE: ca'do, ca'sum, to fall.

cad: -ence, *a falling of the voice;* cascade' (Fr. n.); deca'dence.

cide: ac'cident; coincide' (con + in); coin'cidence; decid'uous; in'cident; oc'cident, *the place of the falling or setting sun, the west.*

case: case, *the state in which a thing happens or falls to be;* casual (Lat. n. *ca'sus,* a fall); cas'ualty; cas'uist, *one who studies cases of conscience;* cas'uistry; occa'sion.

Chance (Fr. v. *choir,* to fall), *something that befalls without apparent cause;* decay (Fr. v. *déchoir,* to fall away).

22. CÆD'ERE: cæ'do, cæ'sum, to cut, to kill.

cide: decide', *to cut off discussion, to determine*; frat'ricide, *the killing of a brother* (Lat. n. *fra'ter*, a brother); hom'icide (*ho'mo*, a man); infan'ticide (*in'fans*, an infant); mat'ricide (*ma'ter*, a mother); par'ricide (*pa'ter*, a father); reg'icide (*rex, re'gis*, a king); su'icide (Lat. pro. *sui*, one's self).

cise: con-, ex-, pre-; concise'ness; decis'ion; deci'sive; excis'ion, incis'ion; inci'sor; precis'ion.

23. CAL'CULUS, a pebble.

calcul: -able (literally, that may be counted by the help of pebbles anciently used in reckoning), -ate, -ation, -ator; incal'culable; miscal'culate.

24. CANDE'RE: can'deo, can'ditum, to be white, to shine (literally, to burn, to glow); Can'didus, white.

cand: -id, *fair, sincere*; -or, *openness, sincerity*; incandes'cent.

can'did: -ate (in Rome aspirants for office wore *white* robes).

Cen'ser, *a vessel in which incense is burned*; in'cense (n.), *perfume given off by fire*; incense' (v.), *to inflame with anger*; incen'diary (Lat. n. *incen'dium*, a fire); can'dle (Lat. *cande'la*, a *white* light made of wax); chand'ler (literally a maker or seller of candles); chandelier'; candel'abra.

25. CAN'ERE: ca'no, can'tum, to sing; Fr chanter, to sing.

cant: cant, *hypocritical sing-song speech*; canta'ta, *a poem set to music*; can'ticle; can'ticles, *the Song of Solomon*; can'to, *division of a poem*; discant'; incanta'tion, *enchantment*; recant', literally, *to sing back, to retract*.

chant: chant; chant'er; chan'ticleer; chant'ry; enchant'.

Ac'cent (Lat. *ad.* and *cantus*, a song), literally, *a modulation of the voice*; accentua'tion; precen'tor (Lat. v. *præcan'ere*, to sing before).

26. CAP'ERE: ca'pio, cap'tum, to take.

cap: -able, -ability; inca'pable.

cip: antic'ipate; eman'cipate (Lat. n. *ma'nus*, hand), literally, *to take away from the hand of an owner, to free*; incip'ient; munic'ipal (Lat. n. *municip'ium*, a free town; *mu'nia*, official duties, and *cap'ere*, to take); partic'ipate (Lat. n. *pars*, *par'tis*, a part); par'ticiple; prince (Lat. n. *prin'ceps*,—Lat. adj. *pri'mus*, first: hence, taking the *first* place or lead); prin'cipal; prin'ciple; recip'ient; rec'ipe (imperative of *recip'ere*; literally, "take thou," being the first word of a medical prescription).

ceive (Fr. root = cap- or cip-): conceive'; deceive'; perceive'; receive'.

capt: -ive, -ivate, -ivity, -or, -ure.

cept: accept' (-able, -ance, -ation); concep'tion; decep'tion; decep'tive; except' (-ion, -ionable); incep'tion; incep'tive; intercept'; pre'cept; precep'tor; recep'tacle; recep'tion; suscep'tible.

ceit (Fr. root = capt- or cept-): conceit'; deceit'; receipt'.

Capa'cious (Lat. adj. *ca'pax*, *capa'cis*, able to hold: hence large); capac'itate; capac'ity; incapac'itate.

CAPUT. (See page 30.)

27. CA'RO, carnis, flesh.

carn: -age, *slaughter*; -al, -ation, *the flesh-colored flower*; incar'nate; incarna'tion.

Carne'lian (Lat. adj. *car'neus*, fleshy), *a flesh-colored stone*; car'nival (Lat. v. *vale*, farewell), *a festival preceding Lent*; carniv'orous (Lat. v. *vora're*, to eat); char'nel (Fr. adj. *charnel*, containing flesh).

28. CAU'SA, a cause.

caus: -al, -ation, -ative; cause (Fr. n. *cause*), n. and v.

Accuse' (Fr. v. *accuser,* to bring a charge against), -ative, -ation, -er; excuse' (Fr. v. *excuser,* to absolve); excus'able; rec'usant (Lat. v. *recusa're,* to refuse).

29. CAVE'RE: ca'veo, cautum, to beware.

caut: -ion, -ious; incau'tious; precaution.

Ca'veat (3d per. sing. present subjunctive = let him beware), *an intimation to stop proceedings.*

30. CA'VUS, hollow.

cav: -ity; concav'ity; ex'cavate.

Cave (Fr. n. *cave*), literally, *a hollow, empty space*; con'cave (Lat. adj. *conca'vus,* arched); cav'il (Lat. n. *cavil'la,* a jest).

31. CED'ERE: ce'do, ces'sum, to go, to yield.

cede: cede; accede'; antece'dent; concede'; precede'; recede'; secede'; unprecedented.

ceed: ex-, pro-, sub- (suc-).

cess: -ation, -ion; ab'scess, *a collection of matter gone away, or collected in a cavity*; ac'cess; acces'sible; acces'sion; acces'sory; conces'sion; excess'; exces'sive; interces'sion; interces'sor; preces'sion; proc'ess; proces'sion; recess'; seces'sion; success' (-ful, -ion, -ive).

32. CENSE'RE: cen'seo, cen'sum, to weigh, to estimate, to tax.

cens: -or, -ure; censo'rious; cen'surable; recen'sion.

Cen'sus (Lat. n. *census,* an estimate).

33. CEN'TRUM, the middle point.

centr: -al, -ical; centrif'ugal (Lat. v. *fu'gere*, to flee); centrip'etal (Lat. v. *pet'ere*, to seek); concen'trate; concentra'tion; concen'tric; eccen'tric; eccentric'ity.

Cen'ter or cen'tre (Fr. n. *centre*), n. and v.; cen'tered.

34. CEN'TUM, a hundred.

cent: cent; cent'age; cen'tenary (Lat. adj. *centena'rius*); centena'rian; centen'nial (Lat. n. *an'nus*, a year); cen'tigrade (Lat. n. *gra'dus*, a degree); cen'tipede (Lat. n. *pes, pe'dis*, the foot); cen'tuple (Lat. adj. *centu'plex*, hundredfold); centu'rion (Lat. n. *centu'rio*, a captain of a hundred); cent'ury (Lat. n. *centu'ria*, a hundred years); percent'age.

35. CER'NERE: cer'no, cre'tum, to sift, to see, to judge; Discrimen, discrim'inis, distinction.

cern: con-, de-, dis-; unconcern'; discern'er, discern'ible, discern'ment.

cret: decre'tal, *a book of decrees*; discre'tion; discre'tionary; excre'tion; se'cret; sec'retary.

discrimin: -ate, -ation; indiscrim'inate.

Decree' (Fr. n. *decret*); discreet' (Fr. adj. *discret*); discrete' (literally, sifted apart), *separate*.

36. CERTA'RE: cer'to, certa'tum, to contend, to vie.

cert: con'cert (n.); concert' (v.); disconcert'; preconcert'.

37. CIN'GERE: cin'go, cinc'tum, to gird.

cinct: cinct'ure; pre'cinct; succinct', literally, *girded or tucked up, compressed, concise*; succinct'ness.

38. CIR'CUS, a circle; cir'culus, a little circle.

circ: cir'cus, *an open space for sports*; cir'clet.

circul: -ar, -ate, -ation, -atory.

Cir'cle (Fr. n. *cercle*); encir'cle; sem'icircle.

39. CITA'RE: ci'to, cita'tum, to stir up, to rouse.

cite: cite, *to summon or quote*; excite' (-able, -ability, -ment); incite' (-ment); recite' (-al); resus'citate (Lat. v. *suscita're*, to raise).

citat: cita'tion; recita'tion; recitative', *a species of musical recitation.*

CIVIS. (See p. 31.)

40. CLAMA'RE: cla'mo, clama'tum, to cry out, to shout; Clam'or, a loud cry.

claim: claim (v. and n., to demand; a demand), ac-, de-, dis-, ex-, pro-, re-; claim'ant; reclaim'a'ble.

clamat: acclama'tion; declama'tion; declam'atory; exclama'tion; exclam'atory; proclama'tion; reclama'tion.

clamor: clam'or (v. and n.), -er, -ous.

EXERCISE.

The *decay* of the tree was caused by the *incisions* which had *accidentally* been made in the bark. The *captives* will be set at liberty, but the *precise* time of their *emancipation* has not been fixed. The harbor is *capacious*, and can *receive* vessels of the largest size. The merits of the *candidates* were *discriminated* with great *candor*. We were *enchanted* with the *carnival* at Rome. This *recitation* is satisfactory. Have you ever seen a *centigrade* thermometer? Nothing is so *successful* as *success*. The number of *concentric circles* in the trunk marked the age of the tree. No *censer* round our altar beams. The heat being *excessive*, we took shelter in the *recesses* of a *cave*. *Precision* is the *principal* quality of good writing. Franklin's father was a tallow *chandler*. Last *century* there was great *carnage* in America.

Infanticide is much practiced in China. The *proclamation* was widely *circulated*. The president was *inaugurated* on the 4th of March. The *census* is taken every ten years. *Conceit* is worse than *eccentricity*. Have you filed your *caveat*?

41. CLAU'DERE: clau'do, clau'sum, to shut, to close.

clud: conclude'; exclude'; include'; preclude'; seclude'.

clus: conclu'sion; conclu'sive; exclu'sion; exclu'sive; recluse'; seclu'sion.

close: close (v., n., adj.); clos'et; close'ness; inclose' (-ure); enclose' (-ure).

Clause (Fr. n. *clause*); clois'ter (old Fr. n. *cloistre*).

42. CLINA'RE: cli'no, clina'tum, to bend; Cli'vus, a slope or hill.

clinat: inclina'tion.

cline: de-, in-, re-.

cliv: accliv'ity; decliv'ity; procliv'ity.

43. COL'ERE: co'lo, cul'tum, to till, to cultivate (Low Lat. Cultiva're, to cultivate).

cult: cult'ure (Lat. n. *cultu'ra*, a cultivation); ag'riculture (Lat. n. *a'ger*, a field); arboricult'ure (Lat. n. *ar'bor*, a tree); flor'iculture (Lat. n. *flos, flo'ris*, a flower); hor'ticulture (Lat. n. *hor'tus*, a garden); ausculta'tion (Lat. n. *ausculta'tio*, a listening; hence, a test of the lungs).

cultiv: -ate, -ation, -ator.

Col'ony (Lat. n. *colo'nia*, a settlement); colo'nial; col'onist; col'onize.

COR. (See page 32.)

CORPUS. (See page 33.)

CREDERE. (See page 35.)

44. CREA'RE: cre'o, crea'tum, to create.

creat: -ion, -ive, -or, -ure; create' (pro-, re-).

45. CRES'CERE: cres'co, cre'tum, to grow.

cresc: cres'cent; excres'cence; decrease'; increase'.

cret: accre'tion; con'crete; concre'tion.

Accrue' (Fr. n. *accrue*, increase); in'crement (Lat. n. *incremen'tum*, increase); recruit' (Fr. v. *recroitre, recru*, to grow again).

46. CRUX, cru'cis, a cross.

cruc: cru'cial (Fr. adj. *cruciale*, as if bringing to the cross: hence, severe); cru'cible (a chemist's melting-pot—Lat. n. *crucib'ulum*—marked in old times with a cross); cru'ciform (Lat. n. *for'ma*, a shape); cru'cify (Lat. v. *fig'ere, fix'um*, to fix); crucifix'ion; excru'ciating.

Cross (Fr. n. *croix*); cro'sier (Fr. n. *crosier*); cruise (Dan. v. *kruisen*, to move crosswise or in a zigzag); crusade' (Fr. n. *croisade*, in the Middle Ages, an expedition to the Holy Land made under the banner of the cross); crusad'er.

47. CUBA'RE: cu'bo (in compos, *cumbo*), cub'itum, to lie down.

cub: in'cubate; incuba'tion; in'cubator.

cumb: incum'bency; incum'bent; procum'bent; recum'bency; recum'bent; succumb' (sub-); superincum'bent.

Cu'bit (Lat. n. *cub'itus*, the elbow, because it serves for leaning upon); in'cubus (Lat. n. *in'cubus*), the nightmare.

48. CU'RA, care.

cur: -able, -ate, -ative, -ator; ac'curate; ac'curacy; inac'curate; proc'urator.

Cu'rious; prox'y (contracted from *proc'uracy*). *authority to act for another;* secure' (Lat. adj. *secu'rus*, from *se* for *si'ne*, without, and *cu'ra*, care); secu'rity; insecure'; si'necure (Lat. prep. *si'ne*, without—an office without duties).

CURRERE. (See page 32.)

49. DA'RE: do, da'tum, to give.

dat: date (originally the time at which a public document was given—*da'tum*); da'ta (Lat. plural of *da'tum*), *facts or truths given or admitted;* da'tive.

dit: addi'tion; condi'tion; ed'it (-ion, -or); perdi'tion; tradi'tion; extradi'tion.

Add (Lat. v. *ad'dere*, to give or put to); adden'dum (pl. adden'da), *something to be added.*

50. DEBE'RE: de'beo, deb'itum, to owe.

debt: debt; debt'or; indebt'ed; deb'it (n. and v.).

51. DE'CEM, ten; Dec'imus, the tenth.

decem: Decem'ber (formerly the *tenth* month); decem'virate (Lat. n. *vir*, a man), *a body of ten magistrates;* decen'nial (Lat. n. *an'nus*, a year).

decim: dec'imal; dec'imate; duodec'imo (Lat. adj. *duodec'imus*, twelfth), *a book having twelve leaves to a sheet.*

52. DENS, den'tis, a tooth.

dent: dent, *to notch;* den'tal; den'tifrice (Lat. v. *frica're*, to rub); den'tist; denti'tion (Lat. n. *denti'tio*, a cutting of the teeth); eden'tate (Lat. adj. *edenta'tus*, toothless); indent'; indent'ure; tri'dent (Lat. adj. *tres*, three), *Neptune's three-pronged scepter;* dan'delion (Fr. *dent-de-lion*, the lion's tooth), *a plant.*

53. DE'US, a God; Divi'nus, relating to God, divine.

de: de'ify; de'ism; de'ist; deist'ical; de'ity.

divin: divine'; divina'tion (Lat. n. *divina'tio,* a foretelling the aid of the gods); divin'ity.

54. DIC'ERE: di'co, dio'tum, to say.

dict: dic'tate; dicta'tor; dictatorial; dic'tion; dic'tionary (Lat. n. *dictiona'rium,* a word-book); dic'tum (pl. dic'ta), *positive opinion;* addict' (Lat. v. *addic'ere,* to devote); benedic'tion (Lat. adv. *be'ne,* well); contradict'; e'dict; indict' (Lat. v. *indic'ere,* to proclaim), *to charge with a crime;* indict'ment; in'terdict; jurid'ic (Lat. n. *jus, ju'ris,* justice), *relating to the distribution of justice;* maledic'tion (Lat. adv. *ma'le,* ill); predict'; predic'tion; valedic'tory (Lat. v. *va'le,* farewell); ver'dict (Lat. adj. *ve'rus,* true).

Dit'to, *n.* (Ital. n. *det'to,* a word), *the aforesaid thing;* indite' (Lat. v. *indic'ere,* to dictate), *to compose.*

55. DI'ES, a day; French jour, a day.

dies: di'al; di'ary; di'et; diur'nal (Lat. adj. *diur'nus,* daily); merid'ian (Lat. n. *merid'ies = me'dius di'es,* midday); merid'ional; quotid'ian (Lat. adj. *quotidia'nus,* daily).

jour: jour'nal; jour'nalist; jour'ney; adjourn'; adjourn'ment; so'journ; so'journer.

DIGNUS (See page 37.)

56. DIVID'ERE: div'ido, divi'sum, to divide, to separate.

divid: divide'; div'idend; subdivide'; individ'ual, literally, *one not to be divided, a single person.*

divis: -ible, -ibility, -ion, -or.

Device' (Fr. n. *devis*, something imagined or devised); devise' (Fr. v. *deviser*, to form a plan).

DOCERE. (See page 38.)

57. DOLE'RE: do'leo, doli'tum, to grieve.

Dole'ful; do'lor; dol'orous; condole'; condo'lence; in'dolent (literally, not grieving or caring), *lazy.*

DOMINUS. (See page 38.)

58. DU'CERE: du'co, duc'tum, to lead, to bring forward.

duc: adduce'; conduce'; condu'cive; deduce'; educe'; ed'ucate; educa'tion; induce'; induce'ment; introduce'; produce'; reduce'; redu'cible; seduce'; superinduce'; traduce'; tradu'cer.

duct: abduc'tion; duc'tile (-ity); conduct' (-or); deduct' (-ion, -ive); induct' (-ion, -ive); introduc'tion; introduc'tory; prod'uct (-ion, -ive); reduc'tion; seduc'tion; seduc'tive; aq'ueduct (Lat. n. *a'qua*, water); vi'aduct (Lat. n. *vi'a*, a road); con'duit (Fr. n. *conduit*), a channel for conveying water.

59. DU'O, two.

du: du'al; du'el (-ist); duet'; du'plicate (Lat. v. *plica're*, to fold); dupli'city (Lat. n. *duplic'itas*, double dealing).

Dubi'ety (Lat. n. *dubi'etas*, uncertainty); du'bious (Lat. adj. *du'bius*, uncertain); indu'bitable (Lat. v. *dubita're*, to doubt); doub'le (Fr. adj. *double*, twofold); doubt (Fr. n. *doubt*), -ful, -less; undoubt'ed.

60. DU'RUS, hard, lasting; DURA'RE: du'ro, dura'tum, to last.

dur: -able, -ableness, -ability, -ance, *state of being held hard and fast;* duresse, *hardship, constraint;* endure' (-ance); ob'duracy.

durat: dura'tion; in'durate, *to grow hard;* indura'tion; ob'duracy.

EXERCISE.

When the speech, was *concluded* loud acclamation *arose*. In many parts of the *colony* much of the waste land has been *reclaimed*, and *agricultural* operations now *receive* the due attention of the *colonists*. The patient declined to undergo *auscultation*. Fishing is a healthful *recreation*. Many of the *crusaders* were inspired with great courage. *Security* was offered, but it was not *accepted*. The *incumbent* could not stand the *crucial* test, and hence *succumbed*. A *curious excrescence* was cut from the tree. To Neptune with his *trident* the Greeks ascribed *divine* power. A French *journalist* has been *indicted*. The *valedictory* was pronounced in *December*. What is the difference between *addition* and *division*? We may easily *predict* the ruin of an *indolent debtor*. How many *maledictions* are heaped on *dentists*! The *reduction* of the public *debt* is desirable. The prisoner was *doleful* because he was in *duresse* vile. An educated man is known by his *accurate* use of language. The *dandelion* is a *productive* plant. The *pilgrims received* the priest's *benediction* before setting out on their *journey*. The *decimal* system *conduces* to the saving of time.

61. EM'ERE: e'mo, emp'tum, to buy or take.

empt: exempt' (-ion); per'emptory (Lat. adj. *perempto'rius*, wholly taken away), *decisive, final*; pre-empt'; pre-emp'tion, *the right of buying before others*; redemp'tion.

Redeem' (Lat. v. *redim'ere*, to buy back); redeem'er; prompt (Lat. adj. *promp'tus = pro-emp'tus*, taken out; hence, ready); prompt'er; prompt'itude; prompt'ness; impromp'tu (Lat. *in promp'tu*, in readiness).

62. ERRA'RE: er'ro, erra'tum, to wander.

err: err, -ant, -antry; er'ror (Lat. n. *er'ror*); erro'neous (Lat. adj. *erro'neus*, erring).

errat: errat'ic; erra'tum (pl. er'rata), *a mistake in printing;* aberra'tion.

63. ES'SE, to be; en, en'tis, being.

ent: ab'sent (-ee); ab'sence; en'tity; nonen'tity; omnipres'ent (Lat. adj. *om'nis*, all); pres'ent (-ation, -ly); represent' (-ation, -ative); misrepresent'.

Es'sence (Lat. n. *essen'tia*, being); essen'tial; quintes'sence (Lat. adj. *quin'tus*, fifth), *the highest essence; in'terest* (3d pers. sing. pres. indic. of *interes'se* = it interests or is of interest); disin'terested.

64. FA'CERE: fa'cio, fac'tum, to do or make; French Faire.

fac: face'tious (Lat. adj. *face'tus*, merry); fac'ile (Lat. adj. *fa'cilis*, easily done); facil'ity; facil'itate; fac'ulty (Lat. n. *facul'tas*, power, ability); fac-sim'ile (Lat. adj. *sim'ilis*, like), literally, *make like, an exact copy*; facto'tum (Lat. adj. *to'tum*, the whole; literally, do the whole), *a servant of all work*.

fic: ben'efice (see *bene*); def'icit (literally, it is wanting), *a lack*; defi'ciency; defi'cient; dif'ficult (Lat. adj. *diffic'ilis*, arduous); ef'ficacy (Lat. adj. *ef'ficax, effica'cis*, powerful); effi'cient, *causing effects*; of'fice (Lat. n. *offic'ium*, a duty); of'ficer; offi'cial; offi'cious; profi'cient; suffice', literally, *to make up what is wanting*; suffi'cient.

fact: fact; fac'tor; fac'tion, *a party acting in opposition*; fac'tious; facti'tious (Lat. adj. *facti'tius*, artificial); benefac'tor; manufacture (Lat. n. *ma'nus*, the hand).

fect: affect' (-ation, -ion); disaffec'tion; confec'tion, literally, *made with sugar* (-er); defect' (-ion, -ive); effect' (-ive); effect'ual; infect' (-ion); infec'tious; per'fect, literally, *thoroughly made* (-ion); imper'fect (-ion); refec'tion; refec'tory.

faire (past participle *fait*): fash'ion (Fr. n. *façon*, the make or form of a thing); fea'sible (Old Fr. *faisible*, that may be done); feat; affair'; coun'terfeit, literally, *to make again, to imitate*; for'feit, (Fr. v. *forfaire*, to misdo), *to lose by some fault*; sur'feit, v., *to overdo in the way of eating*.

65. FAL'LERE: fal'lo, fal'sum, to deceive; French Faillir, to fall short or do amiss.

fall: fal'lacy; falla'cious; fal'lible; fallibil'ity; infal'lible.

fals: false (-hood, -ify); falset'to (Ital. n. = a false or artificial voice).

fail: fail'ure; fault (Old Fr. n. *faulte*); fault'y; fal'ter; default' (-er).

66. FA'NUM, a temple.

fan: fane; fanat'ic (Lat. adj. *fanat'icus*, literally, one inspired by divinity—the god of the fane), *a wild enthusiast*; fanat'ical; fanat'icism; profane', v. (literally, to be before or outside of the temple), *to desecrate*; profane', adj., *unholy*; profana'tion; profan'ity.

67. FA'RI, fa'tus, to speak.

fat: fate, -al, -ality, -alism, -alist; pref'atory.

Affable (Lat. adj. *affab'ilis*, easy to be spoken to); affabil'ity; inef'fable; in'fant (Lat. participle, *in'fans*, *infan'tis*, literally, not speaking) (-ile, -ine); in'fancy; nefa'rious (Lat. adj. *nefa'rius*, impious); pref'ace (Fr. n. *préface*), *something spoken or written by way of introduction.*

68. FATE'RI: fa'teor, fas'sus (in comp. fes'sus), to acknowledge, to show.

fess: confess' (-ion, -ional, -or); profess' (-ion, -ional, -or).

69. FELIX, feli'cis, happy.

felic: -ity, -itous; infeli'city; feli'citate, *to make happy by congratulation.*

70. FEN'DERE: fen'do, fen'sum, to keep off, to strike.[6]

fend: fend (-er); defend' (-er, -ant); offend' (-er).

fens: defense' (-ible, -ive); offense' (-ive); fence (n. and v., abbreviated from defence);[7] fencer; fencing.

71. FER'RE: fe'ro, la'tum, to bear, to carry.

fer: fer'tile (Lat. adj. *fer'tilis*, bearing, fruitful); fertil'ity; fer'tilize; circum'ference, literally, *a measure carried around anything;* confer', *to consult;* con'ference; defer'; def'erence; deferen'tial; dif'fer (-ence, -ent); infer' (-ence); of'fer; prefer' (-able, -ence, -ment); prof'fer; refer' (-ee, -ence); suf'fer (-ance, -able, -er); transfer' (-able, -ence); conif'erous (Lat. n. *co'nus*, a cone); florif'erous (Lat. n. *flos*, *flo'ris*, a flower); fructif'erous (Lat. n. *fruc'tus*, fruit); Lu'cifer (Lat. n. *lux*, *lucis*, light), *the morning or evening star, Satan;* pestif'erous (Lat. n. *pes'tis*, pest, plague).

lat: ab'lative (literally, carrying away; the sixth case of Latin nouns); collate' (-ion); dilate' (-ory); elate'; ob'late, *flattened at the poles;* obla'tion, *an offering;* prel'ate; prel'acy; pro'late, *elongated at the poles;* relate' (-ion, -

ive); correla'tion; correl'ative; super'lative; translate' (-ion); delay' (= dis + lat, through old Fr. verb *delayer,* to put off).

72. FERVE'RE: fer'veo, to boil; Fermen'tum, leaven.

ferv: -ent, -ency, -id, -or; effervesce', *to bubble or froth up;* efferves'cence.

ferment: fer'ment, -ation.

73. FES'TUS, joyful, merry.

fest: -al, -ival, -ive, -ivity; feast (Old Fr. *feste,* a joyous meal); fête (modern Fr. equivalent of *feast), a festival;* festoon (Fr. n. *feston,* originally an ornament for a festival).

74. FID'ERE: fi'do, to trust; Fi'des, faith; Fide'lis, trusty.

fid: confide' (-ant, -ence, -ent, -ential); dif'fidence; dif'fident; per'fidy (per = through and hence *away from* good faith); perfid'ious.

fidel: fidel'ity; in'fidel; infidel'ity.

Fe'alty (Old Fr. n. *féalté* = Lat. *fidel'itas), loy'alty;* fidu'cial (Lat. n. *fidu'cia,* trust); fidu'ciary; affi'ance, *to pledge faith, to betroth;* affida'vit (Low Lat., signifying, literally, he made oath), *a declaration on oath;* defy' (Fr. v. *défier,* originally, to dissolve the bond of allegiance; hence, to disown, to challenge, to brave).

75. FI'GERE: fi'go, fix'um, to join, fix, pierce.

fix: affix'; cru'cifix (Lat. n. *crux, cru'cis,* a cross); cru'cify; fix'ture; post'fix; pre'fix; suf'fix (n., literally, something fixed below or on; hence, appended); transfix', *to pierce through.*

76. FIN'GERE: fin'go, fic'tum, to form, to feign; Figu'ra, a shape.

fict: fic'tion; ficti'tious.

figur: fig'ure; figura'tion; configura'tion; disfig'ure; prefig'ure; transfig'ure.

Feign (Fr. v. *feindre, feignant,* to pretend); feint (*feint,* past part. of *feindre*); ef'figy (Lat. n. *effig'ies,* an image or likeness); fig'ment (Lat. n. *figmen'tum,* an invention).

FINIS. (See page 40.)

77. FIR'MUS, strong, stable.

firm: firm; firm'ness; infirm' (-ary, -ity); fir'mament, originally, *firm foundation;* affirm' (-ation, -ative); confirm' (-ation, -ative).

78. FLAM'MA, a stream of fire.

flam: flame; inflame' (-able, -ation, -atory).

Flambeau' (Fr. n. *flambeau* from v. *flamber,* to blaze); flamin'go (Span. n. *flamenco*), *a bird of a flaming red color.*

EXERCISE.

Age does not always *exempt* one from *faults. Peremptory* orders were given that all the princes should be *present* at the *diet.* Many *beneficial* results must come from the *introduction* of drawing into the public schools. The lady is *affable* and *perfectly* free from *affectation.* The field is *fertile* and *produces* abundant crops. The *professor's* lecture *related* to *edentate* animals. Men sometimes *feign* a *fealty* they do not feel. The lady *professed* that her *felicity* was ineffable. The King seized a *flambeau* with zeal to destroy. It is a *nefarious* act to make a *false affidavit. Fanaticism* is often *infectious.* The *confirmed offender* had issued many *counterfeits.* Dickens gives us the *quintessence* of the *facetious.* In *figure* the earth is an *oblate* spheroid.

79. FLEC'TERE: flec'to, flex'um, to bend.

flect: deflect' (-ion); inflect' (-ion); reflect' (-ion, -ive, -or).

flex: -ible, -ile, -ion, -or (a muscle that bends a joint), -ure; flex'-uous; flex'uose; cir'cumflex; re'flex.

80. FLOS, flo'ris, a flower.

flor: -al, -et, -id, -ist; Flo'ra, *the goddess of flowers*; flor'iculture (Lat. n. *cultu'ra*, cultivation); florif'erous (Lat. v. *fer're*, to bear); flor'in (originally, a Florentine coin with a lily on it); flour (literally, the *flower* or choicest part of wheat); flow'er (-et, -y); flour'ish (Lat. v. *flores'cere*, to begin to blossom, to prosper); efflores'cence; efflores'cent.

FLUERE. (See page 41.)

81. FŒ'DUS, fœd'eris, a league or treaty.

feder: fed'eral; fed'eralist (in the United States a member of the party that favored a strong league of the States); fed'erate; confed'erate; confed'eracy; confedera'tion.

82. FO'LIUM, a leaf.

foli: -aceous, -age, -ate; fo'lio (ablative case of *fo'lium*, a leaf), *a book made of sheets folded once*; exfo'liate, *to come off in scales*; foil, *a thin leaf of metal*; tre'foil, *a plant with three (tres) leaves*; cinque'foil (Fr. *cinque*, five).

83. FOR'MA, shape, form.

form: form (-al, -ality); conform' (-able, -ation, -ity); deform' (-ity); inform' (-ant, -er, -ation); perform' (-ance, -er); reform' (-ation, -atory, -er); transform' (-ation); for'mula (Lat. n. *for'mula*, pl. *for'mulæ*, a little form, a model); for'mulate; mul'tiform (Lat. adj. *mul'tus*, many); u'niform (Lat. adj. *u'nus*, one).

84. FOR'TIS, strong.

fort: fort; for'tress, *a fortified place*; for'tify; fortifica'tion; for'titude; com'fort, n., *something that strengthens or cheers* (-able, -er, -less); discom'fort; effort, *a putting forth of one's strength*; force (Fr. n. *force, strength*); for'cible; enforce' (-ment); reinforce' (-ment).

85. FRAN'GERE: fran'go, frac'tum, to break; Fra'gilis, easily broken.

frang, fring: fran'gible (-ibility); infran'gible; infringe' (-ment); refran'gible.

fract: frac'tion; frac'tious; fract'ure; infract' (-ion); refract' (-ion, -ory).

Fra'gile; frag'ment; frail (old Fr. ad; *fraile* = Lat. *fra'gilis*); frail'ty.

86. FRA'TER, fra'tris, a brother; Frater'nus, brotherly.

fratr: frat'ricide (Lat. v. *cæd'ere*, to kill).

fratern: -al, -ity, -ize; confrater'nity.

Fri'ar (Fr. n. *frère*, a brother); fri'ary.

87. FRONS, fron'tis, the forehead.

front: front (-age, -al, -less, -let); affront'; confront'; effront'ery; fron'tier (Fr. n. *frontière*); front'ispiece (Lat. n. *frontispi'cium*, from *frons* and *spic'ere*, to view; literally, that which is seen in front).

88 FRU'OR: fruc'tus, to enjoy; Fru'ges, corn; French Fruit, fruit.

fruct: -ify, -ification; fructif'erous (Lat. v. *fer're*, to bear).

frug: -al, -ality; frugif'erous (Lat. v. *fer're*, to bear).

fruit: fruit; fruit'erer; fruit'ful; frui'tion.

89. FU'GERE: fu'gio, fu'gitum, to flee.

fug: fuga'cious; centrif'ugal (Lat. n. *cen'trum*, the center); feb'rifuge (Lat. n. *fe'bris*, fever); fugue (Lat. n. *fu'ga*, a flight), *a musical composition*; ref'uge (-ee); sub'terfuge; ver'mifuge (Lat. n. *ver'mis*, a worm).

fugit: fu'gitive (adj. and n.).

90. FU'MUS, smoke.

fum: fume; fu'mid; fumif'erous (Lat. v. *fer're*, to bear), *producing smoke*; fu'matory, *a plant with bitter leaves*; per'fume (-er, -ery).

Fu'migate (Lat. v. *fumiga're, fumiga'tum*, to smoke), *to disinfect*; fumiga'tion; fu'migatory.

91. FUN'DERE: fun'do, fu'sum, to pour.

fund: refund'; found (Fr. v. *fondre* = Lat. *fun'dere*), *to form by pouring into a mould* (-er, -ery); confound' (Fr. v. *confondre*, literally, to pour together; hence, to confuse).

fus: fuse (-ible, -ion); confuse' (-ion); diffuse' (-ion, -ive); effuse' (-ion, -ive); infuse' (-ion); profuse' (-ion); refuse' (-al); suffuse' (-ion); transfuse' (-ion).

92. GER'ERE: ge'ro, ges'tum, to bear or carry.

ger: ger'und, *a Latin verbal noun*; bellig'erent (Lat. n. *bel'lum*, war); con'geries (Lat. n. *conge'ries*, a collection); vicege'rent (Lat. *vi'ce*, in place of), *one bearing rule in place of another*.

gest: gest'ure; gestic'ulate (Lat. n. *gestic'ulus*, a mimic gesture); gesticula'tion; congest' (-ion, -ive); digest', literally, *to carry apart*: hence, *to dissolve food in the stomach* (-ible, -ion, -ive); suggest', literally, *to bear into the mind from below*, that is, *indirectly* (-ion, -ive); reg'ister (Lat. v. *reger'ere*, to carry back, to record); reg'istrar; registra'tion; reg'istry.

93. GIG'NERE: gig'no, gen'itum, to beget; Gens, gen'tis, a clan or nation, Ge'nus, gen'eris, a kind.

genit: gen'itive, *a case of Latin nouns;* congen'ital, *born with one;* primogen'itor (Lat. adj. *pri'mus*, first), *an ancestor;* primogen'iture, *state of being first born;* progen'itor, *an ancestor.*

gent: genteel' (Lat. adj. *genti'lis*, pertaining to the same clan; hence of good family or birth); gentil'ity; gen'tle (*genti'lis*, of good birth), *mild, refined;* gen'try (contracted from gentlery), *a class in English society;* gen'tile, *belonging to a nation other than the Jewish.*

gener: gen'eral (-ity, -ize); gen'erate (Lat. *genera're, genera'tum,* to produce); genera'tion; regenera'tion; gener'ic; gen'erous; generos'ity; con'gener, *of the same kind;* degen'erate, *to fall off from the original kind;* degen'eracy.

Gen'der (Fr. n. *genre* = Lat. *ge'nus, gen'eris*), *the kind of a noun as regards the sex of the object;* gen'ial (Lat. adj. *genia'lis*, cheerful); gen'ius (Lat. n. *ge'nius*, originally, the divine nature innate in everything); gen'uine (Lat. adj. *genui'nus*, literally, proceeding from the original stock; hence, natural, true); ge'nus, a kind including many species; engen'der (Fr. v. *engendrer*, to beget); ingen'ious (Lat. adj. *ingenio'sus*, acute, clever); ingen'uous (Lat. adj. *ingen'uus*, frank, sincere).

94. GRA'DI: gra'dior, gres'sus, to walk.

grad: grada'tion; gra'dient (*gra'diens, gradien'tis,* pres. part. of v. *gradi*), *rate of ascent, grade;* grad'ual (Lat. n. *gradus,* a step); grad'uate; degrade' (-ation); ingre'dient (Lat. part. *ingre'diens*, entering); ret'rograde.

gress: aggres'sion; aggres'sive; con'gress (-ional); digress' (-ion); e'gress; in'gress; prog'ress (-ion, -ive); retrogres'sion; transgress' (-ion, -or).

Grade (Fr. n. *grade* = Lat. *gra'dus*, degree or rank); degree' (Fr. n. *degré* = de + *gradus*).

95. GRA'TUS, thankful, pleasing.

grat: grate'ful; gra'tis (Lat. *gra'tiis*, by favor, for nothing) grat'itude; gratu'ity; gratu'itous; grat'ify (-ication); congrat'ulate (-ion, -ory); ingra'tiate.

Grace (Fr. *grâce* = Lat. *gra'tia*, favor, grace); grace'ful; gra'cious; grace'less; disgrace'; agree' (Fr. v. *agréer*, to receive kindly), -able, -ment; disagree'.

96. GRA'VIS, heavy.

grav: *grave*, literally, *heavy*: hence, *serious*; grav'ity; gravita'tion; ag'gravate (-ion).

Grief (Fr. *grief* = Lat. *gra'vis*), literally, *heaviness of spirit, sorrow*; grieve; griev'ance; griev'ous.

GREX. (See page 41.)

97. HABE'RE: ha'beo, hab'itum, to have or hold; HABITA'RE, hab'ito, habita'tum, to use frequently, to dwell.

habit: habit'ual; habit'uate; hab'itude; hab'itable; hab'itat, *the natural abode of an animal or a plant;* habita'tion; cohab'it; inhab'it (-able, -ant).

hibit: exhib'it, literally, *to hold out, to show* (-ion, -or); inhib'it (-ion); prohib'it (-ion, -ory).

Hab'it (Lat. *hab'itus*, state or dress); habil'iment (Fr. n. *habillement*, from v. *habiller*, to dress); a'ble (Lat. adj. *hab'ilis*, literally, that may be easily held or managed; hence, apt, skillful.)

98. HÆRE'RE: hæ'reo, hæ'sum, to stick.

her: adhere' (-ency, -ent); cohere' (-ence, -ency, -ent); inhere (-ent).

hes: adhe'sion; adhe'sive; cohe'sion; cohe'sive.

Hes'itate (Lat. v. *hæsita're, hæsita'ium*, to be at a stand, to doubt); hes'itancy; hesita'tion.

99. HÆRES, hære'dis, an heir or heiress; French Hériter, to be heir to.

hered: hered'itary, *descending to heirs.*

herit: her'itable; her'itage; inher'it (-ance); disinher'it.

Heir (Old Fr. *heir* = Lat. *hœ'res*); heir'ess; heir'loom (Anglo-Saxon *geloma,* goods).

100. HO'MO, hom'inis, a man; Huma'nus, human.

hom: hom'age (Fr. *hommage,* literally, acknowledgment by a *man* or vassal to his feudal lord); homicide (Lat. v. *cæd'ere,* to kill)

human: hu'man, *belonging to a man*; humane', *having the feelings proper to a man, kind*; human'ity; hu'manize; inhu'man.

EXERCISE.

Floral devices were tastefully *introduced.* The *friar* gives himself to *reflection,* and does not care a *florin* for worldly pleasures. The tree is covered with *foliage,* but bears no *fruit.* The rights of the *fraternity* have been *infringed.* The metal was *fused* in iron pans. By the law of *primogeniture* the eldest son will *succeed* to the estate. *Congress* met, and a *general* of the army was chosen president. The *gradient* is *gentle,* and the *access* easy. The *reform* of the *refractory* was in the highest *degree genuine.* We *received* our *frugal* meal with *gratitude.* Many of the *inhabitants* perished in the *flames.* Hamilton and Jay were leading *federalists.* To err is *human*; to forgive, *divine.* The boy *gesticulated* violently, but it was a mere *subterfuge.* Your words *infuse comfort* into my heart. May one not be *human* without being *humane*? Do you know the *difference* between the *genitive* and the *ablative case*?

101. HU'MUS, the earth; Hu'milis, on the ground, lowly.

hum: exhume' (-ation); inhume.

humil: humil'ity; humil'iate (-ion); hum'ble (Fr. adj. *humble* = Lat. *hu'milis*).

IRE. (See page 41.)

102. JA'CERE: ja'cio, jac'tum, to throw or cast.

ject: ab'ject; ad'jective; conject'ure (-al); deject'ed; dejec'tion; eject' (-ion, -ment); inject' (-ion); interject' (-ion); object' (-ion, -ionable, -ive, -or); project' (-ile, -ion, -or); reject' (-ion); subject' (-ion, -ive); traject'ory.

Ejac'ulate (Lat. v. *ejacula're, ejacula'tum*, to hurl or throw); ejacula'tion; ejac'ulatory; jet (Fr. v. *jéter = ja'cere*); jet'ty; jut.

103. JUN'GERE: jun'go, junc'tum, to join; Ju'gum, a yoke.

junct: junc'tion; junct'ure, *a point of time made critical by a joining of circumstances*; ad'junct; conjunc'tion; conjunc'tive; disjunc'tion; disjunc'tive; injunc'tion; subjunc'tive (literally, joined subordinately to something else).

jug: con'jugal, *relating to marriage;* conjugate (-ion); sub'jugate (-ion).

Join (Fr. v. *joindre* = Lat. *jun'gere*); adjoin'; conjoin'; disjoin'; enjoin'; rejoin'; subjoin'; joint (Fr. part, *joint* = Lat. *junc'tum*); joint'ure, *property settled on a wife, to be enjoyed after her husband's death;* jun'ta (Spanish *junta* = Lat. *junc'tus*, joined), *a grand council of state in Spain;* jun'to (Span, *junt*), *a body of men united for some secret intrigue.*

104. JURA'RE: ju'ro, jura'tum, to swear.

jur: ju'ry; ju'ror; abjure'; adjure'; conjure'; con'jure, *to effect something as if by an oath of magic;* con'jurer; per'jure, *to forswear;* per'jurer; per'jury.

105. JUS, ju'ris, right law; Jus'tus, lawful; Ju'dex, ju'dicis, a judge.

jur: jurid'ical (Lat. v. *dica're*, to pronounce), *relating to the administration of justice;* jurisdic'tion, *legal authority;* jurispru'dence, *science of law;* ju'rist; in'jure; in'jury.

just: just; jus'tice; justi'ciary; jus'tify; justifica'tion.

judic: ju'dicature, *profession of a judge;* judi'cious, *according to sound judgment;* prej'udice, n., *judgment formed beforehand;* prejudi'cial; judge (Fr. n. *juge* = Lat. *ju'dex*); judg'ment; prejudge'.

106. LE'GERE: le'go, lec'tum, to gather, to read.

leg: le'gend (originally, stories of saints to be read—*legen'da*—in church); leg'endary; leg'ible; le'gion (originally, a body of troops *gathered* or levied —*le'gio*); el'egance; el'egant; sac'rilege (originally, the gathering or stealing of something sacred—*sa'crum*).

lig: dil'igent (originally, esteeming highly; hence, assiduous): el'igible; intel'ligible; intel'ligence; intel'ligent; neg'ligent (literally, not—*neg* = *nec* = not—picking up).

lect: lect'ure (-er); collect' (-ion, -ive, -or); recollect' (-ion); eclec'tic (Greek *ec* = *ex*); elect' (-ion, -or, -oral); in'tellect; neglect'; predilec'tion, *a liking for*; select' (-ion); les'son (Fr. n. *leçon* = Lat. *lec'tio*, a reading).

107. LEVA'RE: le'vo, leva'tum, to raise; Le'vis, easily raised, light; French Lever, to rise or raise.

lev: lev'ity; levita'tion; alle'viate (-ion); el'evate (-ion); rel'evant, literally, *raising up:* hence, *pertinent, applicable;* rel'evancy; irrel'evant.

lever: leav'en (Fr. *levain*, yeast); Levant', literally, *the place of the rising sun—the countries near the eastern part of the Mediterranean Sea;* lev'ee; le'ver (-age); lev'y.

LEX. (See page 43.)

108. LI'BER, free.

liber: -al, -ality, -alize, -ate, -ator, -ty.

Deliv'er (Fr. v. *délivrer* = Lat. *delibera're*, to set free); deliv'erance; deliv'ery.

LITERA. (See page 43.)

109. LO'CUS: a place.

loc: -al, -ality, -alize, -ate; locomo'tive (Lat. v. *move're*, to move); al'locate; col'locate (-ion); dis'locate (-ion).

110. LO'QUI: lo'quor, locu'tus, to speak.

loqu: loqua'cious; loqua'city; col'loquy; collo'quial; el'oquent; magnil'oquent (Lat. adj. *mag'nus*, big, pompous); ob'loquy; solil'oquy (Lat. adj. *so'lus*, alone); ventril'oquist (Lat. n. *ven'ter*, the stomach).

locut: circumlocu'tion; elocu'tion; interloc'utor.

111. LU'DERE: lu'do, lu'sum, to play or deceive.

lud: lu'dicrous (Lat. adj. *lu'dicrus*, sportive, laughable); allude', literally, *to play at, to refer to indirectly*; delude'; elude'; prelude'.

lus: allu'sion; collu'sion; delu'sion; delu'sive; illu'sion; prelu'sive; prelu'sory.

112. LUX, lu'cis, light; Lu'men, lu'minis, light.

luc: Lu'cifer (Lat. v. *fer're*, to bear); lu'cid; elu'cidate; translu'cent.

lumin: lu'minary; lu'minous; illu'minate; illu'mine.

113. MAG'NUS, great; Ma'jor, greater; Magis'ter, master.

magn: magnanim'ity (Lat. n. *an'imus*, soul); mag'nate, *a man of rank*; mag'nify (-er); magnif'icent (Lat. v. *fac'ere*, to make), *showing grandeur;*

mag'nitude.

maj: maj'esty (-ic); ma'jor (-ity); may'or; may'oralty.

magister: mag'istrate; mag'istracy; magiste'rial; mas'ter (Old Fr. *maistre* = Lat. *magis'ter);* mis'tress (Old Fr. *maistresse* = Lat *magis'tra,* fem. of *magis'ter*).

114. MA'NUS, the hand; French Main, the hand.

man: man'acle (Lat. n. *man'ica,* a fetter); manip'ulate, *to work with the hand* (-ion, -or); man'ual; manufact'ure (Lat. v. *fac'ere,* to make); manufac'tory; manumit' (Lat. v. *mit'tere,* to send); man'uscript (Lat. v. *scrib'ere, scrip'tum,* to write); amanuen'sis (= *ab + ma'nus), one who does handwriting for another;* eman'cipate (Lat. v. *cap'ere,* to take); quadru'manous (Lat. *quatuor,* four).

main: man'ner (Fr. n. *manière,* originally, the mode in which a thing is *handled*); maneu'ver (Fr. n. *manœuvre,* literally, hand work; Fr. n. *œuvre* = *o'pus,* work); manure', *v.* (contracted from Fr. *manœuvrer,* to cultivate by manual labor).

115. MA'RE, the sea.

Marine' (Lat. adj. *mari'nus,* pertaining to the sea); mar'iner; mar'itime (Lat. adj. *mariti'mus* = *mari'nus*); submarine'; transmarine'; ultramarine'; mermaid (Fr. n. *mer* = Lat. *ma're*).

116. ME'DIUS, the middle.

Mediæ'val (Lat. n. *æ'vum,* age), *relating to the Middle Ages*; me'diate (-ion, -or); me'diocre (Lat. adj. *medio'cris,* middling; hence inferior); medioc'rity; Mediterra'nean (Lat. n. *ter'ra,* land); me'dium (Lat. n. *me'dium,* the middle); imme'diate (prefix *in* = not), *with nothing intervening*; interme'diate.

117. MENINIS'SE: mem'ini, to remember; Me'mor, mindful; MEMORA'RE mem'oro, memora'tum, to remember, to mention.

meminisse: memen'to (imper. mood; literally, *remember thou), a reminder, a memorial.*

memor: mem'orable; memoran'dum (Lat. *memoran'dus*, p. part. of *memora're*; literally, something to be remembered); commem'orate (-ion, -ive); mem'ory (Lat. n. *memo'ria*); memo'rial (-ize); immemo'rial.

Mem'oir (Fr. n. *mémoire* = Lat. *memoran'dum*); men'tion (Fr. n. *mention* = Lat. *men'tio*, a speaking of); remem'ber (Old Fr. v. *remembrer = Lat. remem'orare*); remem'brance; remem'brancer; reminis'cence (Fr. n. *réminiscence*, from Lat. v. *reminis'ci*, to recall to mind).

118. MENS, men'tis, the mind.

ment: men'tal; dement'ed; demen'tia, *insanity*; ve'hement (Lat. adj. *ve'hemens = ve*, not, and *mens*; literally, not reasonable), *furious, ardent.*

EXERCISE.

We *reject* insincere *homage*. When the body was *exhumed* the *jury decided* that poison had been administered. *Legendary* stories were *related* by the *friar*. The *lessons* were *selected* with *intelligence. Levity* and *gravity* are *different* qualities. The *mayor's* speech was more *ludicrous* than *facetious*. The *magistrate* claimed *jurisdiction* in the *locality*. We heard Hamlet's *soliloquy* finely *delivered*. Do you *recollect* the *magnificent* lines at the beginning of "Paradise Lost"? The *lecturer* was *lucid* in his *allusions*. In *mediæval* times *homage* was exacted of all vassals. The *mariners maneuvered* beautifully. Your *magnificent donation* will be *gratefully remembered*. The *mermaid* is a mere *delusion. Illegible manuscript* is a *decided nuisance*. The eastern part of the *Mediterranean* is called the *Levant*. Franklin's *memoirs* are very interesting.

119. MER'CES, hire; Merx, mer'cis, merchandise.

merc: mer'cantile (Lat. part. *mer'cans, mercan'tis*); mer'cenary (Lat. adj. *mercena'rius*); mer'cer (Fr. n. *mercier), one who deals in silks and woolens*; mer'chant (Lat. part, *mer'cans*); mer'chandise; com'merce (Fr. n.

commerce); commer'cial; mar'ket (Lat. n. *merca'tus*, a place of public traffic).

120. MER'GERE: mer'go, mer'sum, to dip, to sink.

merg: merge; emerge'; emer'gency, *that which arises suddenly;* submerge'.

mers: emer'sion; immerse'.

121. MIGRA'RE: migro, migra'tum, to remove.

migr: em'igrant (Lat. part. *mi'grans, migran'tis*).

migrat: mi'grate (-ion, -ory); em'igrate (-ion); im'migrate (-ion); transmigra'tion, *the passage of the soul into another body after death.*

122. MI'LES, mil'itis, a soldier.

milit: -ary, -ant; mil'itate, *to act against;* mili'tia, *enrolled soldiers not in a standing army.*

123. MINE'RE: min'eo, min'itum, to hang over.

min. em'inent (Lat. part, *em'inens,* standing out); em'inence; im'minent, literally, *threatening to fall;* pre-em'inent; pre-em'inence; prom'inent; prom'inence; superem'inent.

124. MINU'ERE: min'uo, minu'tum, to lessen; Mi'nor, less; Mi'nus, less.

minut: minute'; minu'tiæ (pl. of Lat. n. *minu'tia,* a very small object); min'uend (Lat. part, *minuen'dus,* to be lessened); min'uet (Fr. n. *minuet* = Lat. adj. *minu'tus,* small), *a dance of small steps;* dimin'ish (Lat. v. *diminu'ere,* to lessen); diminu'tion; dimin'utive.

minor: mi'nor, *n.* and *a.;* minor'ity.

minus: mi'nus (Lat. adj. comp. deg., less); min'imum (Lat. adj. super, deg., least); min'im.

125. MINIS'TER, a servant or attendant.

minister: min'ister; ministe'rial; min'istry; admin'ister; administra'tion; admin'istrative; administra'tor.

126. MIRA'RI: mi'ror, mira'tus, to wonder.

mir: admire' (-able, -ation); mir'acle (Lat. n. *mirac'ulum,* a wonderful thing); mirac'ulous.

Mirage' (Fr. n. *mirage,* a reflection); mir'ror (Fr. n. *miroir,* from v. *mirer,* to view).

127. MISCE'RE: mis'ceo, mix'tum, to mingle.

misc: mis'cellany; miscella'neous; promis'cuous.

mixt: mix; mixt'ure; admixt'ure; intermix'.

128. MI'SER, wretched.

miser: mi'ser (-able); mis'ery; commis'erate (-ion).

129. MIT'TERE: mit'to, mis'sum, to send or cast.

mit: admit' (-ance); commit' (-ee, -ment); demit'; emit'; intermit' (-ent); manumit' (Lat. n. *manus,* the hand), *to release from slavery;* omit'; permit'; pretermit'; remit' (-ance); submit'; transmit'; mit'timus (Lat. *we send*), *a warrant of commitment to prison.*

miss: mis'sile; mis'sion (-ary); admis'sible; admis'sion; com'missary, *an officer who furnishes provisions for an army;* commissa'riat; commis'sion (-er); com'promise; demise', *death;* em'issary; intermis'sion; omis'sion;

permis'sion; premise'; prem'ises; prom'ise (-ory); remiss' (-ion); submis'sion; submis'sive; transmis'sion; transmis'sible.

130. MODERA'RI: mod'eror, modera'tus, to keep within bounds; Mo'dus, a measure or manner.

moderat: mod'erate (-ion, -or); immod'erate.

mod: mode; mood; mod'ify (-able, -er); modifica'tion; accom'modate (-ion); commode' (Lat. adj. *com'modus*, convenient). *a small sideboard*; commo'dious, literally, *measured with*; commod'ity, literally, *a convenience*; incommode'; mod'ern (Lat. adv. *mo'do*, lately, just now); mod'ernize; mod'ulate (Lat. n. *mod'ulus*, a measuring of tones); modula'tion.

131. MONE'RE: mo'neo, mon'itum, to remind, to warn.

mon: admon'ish; mon'ument (Lat. n. *monumen'tum*); premon'ish; sum'mon (Lat. v. *summone're* = *sub* + *mone're*, to remind privily), *to call by authority*.

monit: mon'itor (-ial); admoni'tion; admon'itory; premoni'tion; premon'itory.

132. MONS, mon'tis, a mountain.

mount: mount, n. *a high hill*; v. *to rise or ascend*; moun'tain (-eer, -ous); mount'ebank (It. n. *banco*, a bench); amount'; dismount'; par'amount (Fr. *par* = Lat. *per*, exceedingly), *of the highest importance*; prom'ontory (literally, the *fore*-part or projecting part of a mountain); remount'; surmount' (-able); tan'tamount (Lat. adj. *tan'tus*, so much); ultramon'tane (literally, beyond the Alps; i. e. on the Italian side).

133. MONSTRA'RE: mon'stro, monstra'tum, to point out, to show.

monstr: mon'ster; mon'strous; monstros'ity; mus'ter, literally, *to show up, to display*.

monstrat: dem'onstrate (-able, -ion, -ive); remon'strate; remon'strance.

134. MORDE'RE: mor'deo, mor'sum, to bite.

mord: mor'dant, *biting, serving to fix colors*; morda'cious (Lat. adj. *mor'dax, morda'cis*, biting), *severe, sarcastic.*

mors: mor'sel, literally, *a little bite*; remorse', *the biting of conscience* (-ful, -less).

MORS. (See page 44.)

135. MOS, mo'ris, manner, custom; pl. Mo'res, manners or morals.

mor: mor'al (ist, -ity, -ize); immor'al (-ity); demor'alize (-ation).

136. MOVE'RE: mo'veo, mo'tum, to move.

mov: move (-able, -er, -ment); remove' (-able, -al).

mot: (-ive, -or); commo'tion; emo'tion (-al); locomo'tion (Lat. n. *lo'cus*; a place); promote' (-er, -ion); remote' (-ness).

Mob (Lat. adj. *mob'ilis*, easily moved); mo'bile (-ity); momen'tum, *the force of a moving body, impetus.*

137. MUL'TUS, multi, many, much.

multi: mul'titude; multitu'dinous; multifa'rious; mul'tiform; mul'tiple (Lat. adj. *mul'tiplus* for *mul'tiplex*, manifold); mul'tiply (Lat. adj. *mul'tiplex*); mul'tiplicate (-ion); multiplic'ity.

138. MU'NUS, mu'neris, a gift, a service.

mun. munic'ipal (Lat. n. *municip'ium*, a free town), *pertaining to a corporation*; municipal'ity; munif'icent; munif'icence; com'mon (Lat. adj. *commu'nis = con + munus*; literally, ready to be of service); commune', *v.*

literally, *to share (discourse) in common*; commun'ion, commu'nity; com'munism; com'munist; commun'icate (-ion, -ive); commu'nicant; excommu'nicate; immu'nity (*in* + *munus*; literally, absence of service).

muner: remunerate (-ion, -ive).

139. MUTA'RE: mu'to, muta'tum, to change.

mut: mu'table (-ity); immu'table; commute'; transmute' (-able).

mutat: muta'tion; commutation; transmuta'tion.

140. NAS'CI: nas'cor, na'tus, to be born, to grow; Natu'ra, nature.

nasc: nas'cent, *growing*; renaissance' (a style of decorative art *revived* by Raphael).

nat: na'tal; na'tion, originally, *a distinct race or stock* (-al, -ality, -ize); interna'tional; na'tive (-ity); cog'nate; in'nate.

natur: nat'ural (-ist, -ize, -ization); preternat'ural; supernat'ural.

141. NA'VIS, a ship.

nav: nave, *the middle or body of a church*; na'val; na'vy; nau'tical (Lat. adj. *nau'ticus*, from *nauta* or *nav'ita*, a sailor); nav'igate (Lat. v. *naviga're* = *na'vis* + *ag'ere*); nav'igable; naviga'tion; nav'igator; circumnavigate.

142. NEC'TERE: nec'to, nex'um, to tie or bind.

nect: connect' (-ion, -ive); disconnect' (-ion).

nex: annex'; annexation.

EXERCISE.

The *administration* of affairs is in the hands of her *majesty's ministers*. A *miscellaneous collection* of goods was sold on *commission*. The *merchant remitted* the money called for in the *emergency*. The *suggestion* to *modify* the plan was *tantamount* to its *rejection*. Do you *admire* Bunker Hill Monument? A *miser* is an object of *commiseration* to all who know him. *Remuneration* will be allowed according to the *amount* of labor. The *major* has been *promoted* to the rank of colonel. All who were *connected* with the *movement* were *excommunicated*. As the *annexed* territory is chiefly *maritime* it will greatly *increase* the *commerce* of the *nation*. The *monitor admonished* the pupils with great *gentleness*. The *committee* said the *master* had done his work in an *admirable* manner. The *Pilgrim* Fathers *emigrated* to this country in 1620. A *minute missile moved* towards us. What is the *subjunctive mood* or *mode*? A *multitude* of *communists* appeared in Paris.

143. NEGA'RE: ne'go, nega'tum, to deny.

negat: nega'tion; neg'ative; ab'negate (-ion); ren'egade, *an apostate*.

Deny' (Fr. v. *dénier* = Lat. *de* + *nega're*, to contradict); deni'al; undeni'able.

144. NEU'TER, neu'trum, neither of the two.

neutr: neu'ter; neu'tral (-ity, -ize).

145. NOCE'RE: no'ceo, no'citum, to hurt.

noc: no'cent, *hurtful*; in'nocent; in'nocence; innoc'uous.

Nox'ious (Lat. adj. *nox'ius*, hurtful); obnox'ious; nui'sance (Fr. v. *nuire* = Lat. *noce're*).

146. NO'MEN, nom'inis, a name.

nomen: nomenclat'ure, *a list of technical names*; cogno'men, *a surname*.

nomin: nom'inal; nom'inate (-ion, -ive); nominee'; denom'inate (-ion, -or); ig'nominy (Lat. *i(n)* + *gnomen*, old form of *nomen*, a deprivation of one's good name); ignomin'ious.

Noun (Fr. n. *nom* = Lat. *no'men*); pro'noun; misno'mer (Old Fr. *mes* = wrong, and *nommer*, to name), *a wrong name*.

NORMA. (See page 45.)

147. NOS'CERE: nos'co, no'tum, to know; No'ta, a mark.

not: note (-able, -ary, -ice, -ify, -ion); no'ticeable; notifica'tion; noto'rious (Lat. adj. *noto'rius*, making known), *known in a bad sense*; notori'ety; an'notate (-ion); denote'.

No'ble (Lat. adj. *no'bilis*, deserving to be known); noblesse' (Fr. n. *noblesse* = Lat. *nobil'itas*); nobil'ity; enno'ble; igno'ble (Lat. prefix *i(n)* + *gnobilis*, old form of *nobilis*); cog'nizance (Old Fr. *cognizance* = Lat. *cognoscen'tia*, notice or knowledge), *judicial observation*; connoisseur' (Fr. n. *connoisseur*, a critical judge); incog'nito (Italian *incognito*, from Lat. part. *incog'nitus*, unknown), *unknown*, *in disguise*; rec'ognize (Lat. *re*, again, and *cognos'cere*, to know); recog'nizance, *a term in law*; recogni'tion; reconnoi'ter (Fr. v. reconnoitre), *to survey, to examine*.

148. NO'VUS, new.

nov: in'novate (-ion, -or); ren'ovate (-ion, -or).

Nov'el (Lat. adj. *novel'lus*, diminutive of *no'vus*); adj. *something new, out of the usual course*; n., literally, *a story new and out of the usual course*; nov'elist; nov'elty; nov'ice, *a beginner*; novi'tiate, *time of being a novice*.

149. NU'MERUS, a number.

numer: (-al, -ate, -ation, -ator, -ic, -ical, -ous); enu'merate (Lat. v. *enumera're, enumera'tum*, to count or tell of), *to reckon up singly*; enumera'tion; innu'merable (= *in* + *nu'mer* + *able*, that may not be counted); supernu'merary, *one above the necessary number*; num'ber (Old Fr. n. *numbre* = Lat. *nu'merus*).

150. NUNCIA'RE: nuncio, nuncia'tum, to announce; Nun'cius, a messenger.

nunciat: enun'ciate, *to utter* (-ion); denuncia'tion; pronuncia'tion; renuncia'tion, *disavowal, relinquishment.*

Nun'cio (Sp. n. *nuncio* = Lat. *nun'cius), a messenger from the Pope*; announce' (Fr. v. *annoncer* = Lat. *ad* + *nuncia're), to proclaim*; announce'ment; denounce' (Fr. v. *dénoncer* = Lat. *de* + *nuncia're), to accuse publicly*; pronounce' (Fr. v. *prononcer* = Lat. *pro* + *nuncia're*); pronounce'able; renounce' (Fr. v. *renoncer* = Lat. *re* + *nuncia're), to disclaim*; renounce'ment.

151. NUTRI'RE: nu'trio, nutri'tum, to nourish.

nutri: nu'triment, *that which nourishes*; nutri'tion; nutri'tious; nu'tritive.

Nour'ish (Fr. v. *nourrir* = Lat. *nutri'ere*); nurse (Fr. v. *nourrice*; a nurse); nur'sery; nurs'ling, *a little one who is nursed*; nurt'ure.

152. O'PUS, op'eris, a work or deed; OPERA'RI, opera'tus, to work.

oper: operose, *requiring labor, tedious.*

operat: operate (-ion, -ive, -or); co-operate (-ion, -ive, -or).

Op'era (It. *op'era* = *opera*, pains, pl. of *o'pus), a musical drama*; operat'ic.

ORDO. (See page 45.)

153. PAN'DERE: pan'do, pan'sum, and pas'sum, to spread; Pas'sus, a step.

pand: expand', *to spread out.*

pans: expanse' (-ion, -ive).

pass: pass; pass'able, *that may be passed, tolerable*; pas'sage; com'pass, v. *to stretch round*; encom'pass; surpass'; tres'pass (*tres* = *trans*), *to pass beyond due bounds.*

Pace (Fr. n. *pas* = Lat. *pas'sus*); pas'senger (Old Eng. *passager*); pass'over, *a Jewish festival*;[8] pass'port (= pass + port, literally, a permission to leave a port or to sail into it.)

154. PAR, equal.

par: par'ity; dispar'ity; dispar'age, *to injure by comparison of unequals*; dispar'agement.

Pair (Fr. adj. *paire* = Lat. *par*), *two of a kind*; peer (Old Fr. *peer* or *pair* = Lat. *par*), *an equal, a nobleman*; peer'age; peer'less; compeer'; non'pareil (Fr. *non*, not, and *pareil*, equal), *a peerless thing or person.*

155. PARA'RE. pa'ro, para'tum, to make ready, to prepare; SEPARA'RE: sep'aro, separa'tum, to separate.

parat: compar'ative; prepara'tion; prepar'atory; repara'tion.

separ: sep'arate, literally, *to prepare aside*: hence, *to disjoin*; separa'tion; sep'arable; insep'arable.

Parade' (Fr. n. *parade*, literally, a parrying), *military display*; pare (Fr. v. *parer*, to pare or ward off); par'ry (Fr. v. *parer*, to ward off); appara'tus (Lat. *appara'tus* = ad + paratus, literally, something prepared for a purpose); appar'el (Fr. n. *appareil*, preparation); compare' (Fr. v. *comparer* = Lat. *compara're*), *to set things together to see how far they resemble each other*; prepare' (Fr. v. *preparer* = Lat. *prepara're*); repair' (Fr. v. *réparer* = Lat. *repara're*), literally, *to prepare again*, hence, *to restore after injury*; irrep'arable; sev'er (Old Fr. v. *sevrer* = Lat. *separa're*), *to render asunder*; sev'eral (Old Fr. adj. *several* = Lat. *separa'lis*, separate); sev'erance; dissev'er.

PARS. (See page 46.)

156. PAT'ER, pa'tris, a father; Pa'tria, one's native country.

Pater'nal (Lat. adj. *pater'nus*, pertaining to a father); pater'nity (Lat. n. *pater'nitas*, Fr. *paternité*), *fathership*; patri'cian (Lat. adj. *patri'cius*, from *pa'tres*, fathers or senators), *a Roman nobleman*; pat'rimony (Lat. n. *patrimo'nium*), *an estate inherited from one's ancestors*; pa'tron (Lat. n. *patro'nus*, a protector), *one who countenances or supports*; pat'ronage; pat'ronize; pat'tern (Fr. n. *pattern*, something to be copied), *a model*; expatriate, *to banish*; expatria'tion.

157. PA'TI: pa'tior, pas'sus, to bear, to suffer.

pati: pa'tient; pa'tience; impa'tient; compat'ible, *consistent with*; compat'ibility; incompat'ible.

pass: pas'sion, *strong agitation of the mind*; pas'sive; impas'sive, *insensible*; compas'sion, *sympathy*; compas'sionate.

158. PEL'LERE; pel'lo, pul'sum, to drive.

pel (com-, dis-, ex-, im-, pro-, re-).

puls: pulse, *the beating of an artery as blood is driven through it*; pul'sate; pulsa'tion; compul'sion; compul'sory; expul'sion; propul'sion; repulse'; repul'sive.

159. PENDE'RE; pen'deo, pen'sum, to hang.

pend: pen'dant, *a long, narrow flag*; pend'ing, *not decided, during*; append'; append'age; depend' (-ant, -ent, -ence); independ'ent; independ'ence; suspend'.

pens: pen'sile, *hanging*; suspense'(-ion).

Pen'dulous (Lat. adj. *pen'dulus*, hanging); pen'dulum (Lat. adj. *pen'dulus)*; appen'dix (Lat. n. *appen'dix*, an addition).

160. PEN'DERE: pen'do, pen'sum, to weigh, to pay.

pend: com'pend (contraction of compendium); compen'dium (Lat. n. *compen'dium,* that which is weighed, saved, shortened); compen'dious (Lat. adj. *compendio'sus,* brief, succinct); expend'; expen'diture; sti'pend (Lat. n. *stipen'dium,* literally, the pay of soldiers); stipendiary.

pens: pen'sive, *thoughtful;* pen'sion, *an allowance for past services* (-eer); com'pensate (-ion); dispense', *to deal out* (-ary); dispensa'tion; indispen'sable; expense' (-ive); rec'ompense.

<h2 style="text-align:center">PES. (See page 47.)</h2>

161. PET'ERE: pe'to, peti'tum, to attack, to seek.

pet: centrip'etal (Lat. n. *cen'trum,* center); compete'; com'petent, *fit, suitable;* com'petence, *sufficiency;* incom'petent.

petit: peti'tion, *a request* (-er); compet'itor; compet'itive; repeti'tion.

Pet'ulant (Fr. adj. *petulant,* fretful); ap'petite (Fr. n. *appétit*), *a seeking for hunger;* impet'uous (Lat. adj. *impetuo'sus,* vehement); impetuos'ity; im'petus (Lat. n. *im'petus,* a shock); repeat' (Fr. v. *répéter* = Lat. *repet'ere*).

<h2 style="text-align:center">EXERCISE</h2>

Numerous objections were *submitted* against the *innovations* about to be *introduced.* The *obnoxious* articles have been *removed.* The *nominee* by his *ludicrous* speech *neutralized* all that his friends did for him. *Part* of the *apparatus prepared* for the *occasion* was damaged in *transmission.* The *patronage* of the *nobility* and *gentry connected* with the neighborhood was asked. Many *parts* of the *edifice* are highly *ornate.* Christ had *compassion* on the *multitude,* for they had been a long time without food. The *petitioner's application* for a *pension* was not *repeated.* How can an *acid* be *neutralized?* The *renegade* was brought to *ignominy.* The *prince* was travelling *incognito.* The young lady seems *pensive* rather than *petulant.* Here is a new *edition* of the *novel,* with *annotations* by the *author.* The *opera* seems to be well *patronized* this winter. Webster had a *compendious mode* of stating great truths. What is meant by *centripetal motion?* What is the *difference* between the *numerator* and the *denominator?*

162. PLEC'TERE: plec'to, plex'um, to twist; PLICA'RE: pli'co, plica'tum, and plic'itum, to fold.

plex: com'plex (literally, twisted together); complex'ion; complex'ity; perplex' (literally, to twist thoroughly—*per*: hence, to puzzle or embarrass); perplex'ity.

plic: ap'plicable (-ity); ap'plicant; ex'plicable.

plicat: applica'tion; com'plicate (-ion); du'plicate; im'plicate (-ion); replica'tion, *an answer in law*; sup'plicate, *to entreat earnestly*; supplica'tion.

plicit: explic'it (literally, out-folded; hence, distinctly stated); implic'it, *implied*.

Ply (Fr. v. *plier* = Lat. *plica're*), *to work diligently*; pli'able, *easily bent*; pli'ant; pli'ancy; accom'plice, *an associate in crime*; apply' (Old Fr. *applier* = Lat. *applica're*); appli'ance, *the thing applied*; comply' (Fr. v. *plier*), *to fold with*: hence, *to conform or assent*; compli'ance; display' (Old Fr. v. *desployer*, to unfold); doub'le (Fr. adj. *double* = Lat. *du'plex*, twofold); du'plex; duplic'ity (Lat. n. *duplic'itas*, from *du'plex*, double); employ' (Fr. v. *employer* = Lat. *implica're*), *to keep at work*; employé; employ'er; employ'ment; exploit' (Fr. n. *exploit* = Lat. *explic'itum*, literally, something unfolded, set forth: hence, a deed, an achievement); imply', literally, *to infold*: hence *to involve, to signify*; mul'tiply (Fr. v. *multiplier* = Lat. *mul'tus* much, many); quad'ruple (Lat. *qua'tuor*, four); reply' (Old Fr. v. *replier* = Lat. *replica're*, to answer); sim'ple (Lat. *simplex*, gen. *simplicis*), *not compounded, artless*; sim'pleton (compare It. *simplicione*, a silly person); simplic'ity (Lat. n. *simplic'itas*); sim'plify; sup'ple (Fr. adj. *souple* = Lat. *sup'plex*, bending the knee, from *sub* and *plica're*); sup'pliant (literally, bending the knees under, kneeling down); treb'le (Old Fr. adj. *treble* = Lat. *tri'plex*, threefold); trip'le (Lat. *tri'plex*); trip'let, *three lines rhyming alternately*.

163. PON'ERE: po'no, pos'itum, to place.

pon: compo'nent, *forming a compound*; depone', *to bear testimony*; depo'nent; oppo'nent; postpone' (-ment).

posit: posi'tion; pos'itive; pos'itivism, *a system of philosophy*; pos'itivist, *a believer in the positive philosophy*; ap'posite, *adapted to*; compos'ite, *compound*; composi'tion; compos'itor; decomposi'tion; depos'it (-ary, -ion, -ory); deposi'tion, *the giving testimony under oath*; exposi'tion; expos'itor; imposi'tion; interposi'tion; juxtaposi'tion; op'posite (-ion); preposi'tion; proposi'tion; supposi'tion; suppositi'tious; transposi'tion.

Pose (Fr. v. *poser* = Lat. *pon'ere*), *to bring to a stand by questions*; post; post'age; post'ure (Fr. n. *posture* = Lat. *positu'ra*, position); compose' (Fr. v. *composer* = Lat. *compon'ere*); compos'ure; com'pound (Lat. v. *compon'ere*); com'post, *a mixture, a manure*; depot' (Fr. n. *dépôt* = Lat. *depos'itum*); dispose' (Fr. v. *disposer*); dispo'sal; expose' (Fr. v. *exposer*); expos'ure; impose' (Fr. v. *imposer*); im'post, *a tax placed on imported goods*; impos'tor, *one guilty of fraud*; impost'ure; interpose'; oppose'; propose'; prov'ost (Old Fr. *provost*, from Lat *præpos'itus*, placed before, a chief), *the principal of a college*; pur'pose (Old Fr. n. *purpos, propos* = Lat. *propos'itum*), *an end set before one*; repose' (Fr. v. *reposer*); suppose' (Fr. v. *supposer*); transpose' (Fr. v. *transposer*).

164. PORTA'RE: por'to, porta'tum, to carry.

port: port'able; por'ter (-age); deport'ment; export' (-ation, -er); im'port (-ance, -ant, -er); pur'port, *design*; report' (-er); support'; insupport'able; transport' (-ation).

Portfo'lio (Lat. n. *fo'lium*, a leaf); portman'teau (Fr. n. *manteau*, a cloak); importune' (Lat. adj. *importu'nus*, unseasonable); import'unate; importu'nity; op'portune (Lat. adj. *opportu'nus*, literally, at or before the port or harbor: hence, seasonable); opportu'nity; inop'portune.

165. POS'SE, to be able; Po'tens, poten'tis, powerful, mighty.

posse: pos'sible (Lat. adj. *possib'ilis*); possibil'ity; impos'sible.

potent: po'tent; po'tency; po'tentate; poten'tial; im'potent; omnip'otent (Lat. adj. *om'nis*, all); plenipoten'tiary (Lat. adj. *ple'nus*, full).

166. PREHEN'DERE: prohen'do, prehen'sum, to lay hold of, to seize.

prehend: apprehend'; comprehend'; reprehend'.

prehens: prehen'sile; apprehen'sion; apprehen'sive; comprehen'sible; comprehen'sion; comprehen'sive; reprehen'sible.

Appren'tice (Old Fr. n. *apprentis*, from v. *apprendre*, to learn); apprise' (Fr. v. *apprendre*, part. *appris*, to inform); comprise' (Fr. v. *comprendre*, *compris*), *to include*; en'terprise (Fr. n. *entrepise*, something undertaken); impreg'nable (Fr. adj. *imprenable*, not to be taken); pris'on (Fr. n. *prison*); prize (Fr. n. *prise*, something taken, from *prendre*, *pris*, to take); reprieve' (Old Fr. v. *repreuver*, to condemn), *to grant a respite*; repri'sal; surprise'.

167. PREM'ERE: pre'mo, pres'sum, to press.

press: press (-ure); compress' (-ible); depress' (-ion); express' (-ion, -ive); impress' (-ion, -ive, -ment); irrepres'sible; oppress' ('-ion, -ive, -or); repress' (-ion, -ive); suppress' (-ion).

Print (abbreviated from *imprint*, from Old Fr. v. *preindre* = Lat. *prem'ere*); im'print, *the name of the publisher and the title page of a book*; imprima'tur (Lat. *let it be printed*), originally, *a license to print a book, the imprint of a publisher*.

168. PRI'MUS, first; Prin'ceps, prin'cipis, chief, original.

prim: prime; pri'mate, *the highest dignitary of a church*; pri'macy; prim'ary; primer; prime'val (Lat. n. *æ'vum*, an age); prim'itive; primogen'itor (Lat. n. *gen'itor*, a begetter); primogeniture (Lat. n. *genitu'ra*, a begetting), *the exclusive right of inheritance which in English law belongs to the eldest son or daughter*; primor'dial (Lat. v. *ordi'ri*, to begin), *existing from the beginning*; prim'rose (Lat. n. *ro'sa*); prin'cess; prince (Fr. n. *prince* = Lat. *prin'ceps*); prin'cipal; prin'ciple.

Pre'mier (Fr. adj. *premier*, first), *the prime minister*; pri'or (Lat. adj. *prior*, former); pri'oress, *the female superior of a convent*; pri'ory, *a convent*; prior'ity, *state of being first*; pris'tine (Lat. adj. *pristi'nus*, primitive), *original, ancient.*

169. PROBA'RE: pro'bo, proba'tum, to try, to prove.

prob: prob'able, *likely, credible*; probabil'ity; improb'able; pro'bate, *the proof of a will*; proba'tion, *the act of trying*; proba'tioner; proba'tionary; probe, *to try by an instrument*; prob'ity, *tried integrity*; approba'tion, *commendation*; rep'robate (adj. literally, proved against), *base, condemned.*

Prove (Old Fr. *prover*, New Fr. *prouver* = Lat. *proba're*); proof (Old Fr. n. *prove* = Lat. *pro'ba*, proof); approve' (Fr. v. *approuver* = Lat. *approba're*); approv'al; disapprove'; improve', (-ment); reprove'; reproof'.

170. PUN'GERE: pun'go, punc'tum, to prick; Punc'tum, a point.

pung: pun'gent; pun'gency; expunge', *to mark out.*

punct: punctil'io (Sp. *punctillo*, from Lat. *punc'tum*, a point), *a nice point of exactness in conduct*, etc.; punctil'ious; punct'ual (-ity); punct'uate (-ion); punct'ure; compunc'tion, *remorse.*

Punch (abbreviated from *puncheon*, from Lat. n. *punc'tio*, a pricking), *an instrument for cutting holes*; point (Fr. n. *pointe* = Lat. *punc'tum)*; poign'ant (Fr. part. *poignant*, stinging); pon'iard (Fr. n. *poignard*), *a small dagger.*

171. PUTA'RE: pu'to, puta'tum, to think, to prune, to count or reckon.

put: compute' (-able, -ation); depute' (Lat. v. *deputa're*, to allot), *to empower to act*; dep'uty; dispute' (-ant); indis'putable; impute' (literally, to reckon in), *to charge*; repute'; disrepute' (-able).

putat: pu'tative, *supposed*; am'putate, *to cut off the limb from an animal*; deputa'tion; imputa'tion; reputa'tion.

Count (Fr. v. *compter* = Lat. computa're); account'; discount'; recount'.

172. RAP'ERE: ra'pio, rap'tum, to seize suddenly, to snatch or hurry away.

rap: rapa'cious (Lat. adj. *ra'pax, rapa'cis,* greedy); rapac'ity; rap'id (Lat. adj. *rap'idus,* swift); rapid'ity; rap'ids; rap'ine (Lat. n. *rapi'na,* robbery).

rapt: rapt, *transported;* rapt'ure (-ous); enrapt'ure; surrepti'tious (Lat. v. *surrip'ere, surrep'tum,* to take away secretly), *done by stealth.*

Rav'age (Fr. v. *ravager* = to lay waste); rav'ish (Fr. v. *ravir* = Lat. *rap'ere*).

173. REG'ERE: re'go, rec'tum, to rule; Rec'tus, straight.

reg: re'gent; re'gency; reg'imen (Lat. n. *reg'imen,* that by which one guides or governs anything); reg'iment (Lat. n. *regimen'tum*); re'gion (Lat. *re'gio, regio'nis,* a region); cor'rigible (Lat. v. *corrig'ere* = *con* + *reg'ere*); incor'rigible.

rect: rec'tify; rec'titude; rec'tor (-ory); correct' (Lat. v. *corrig'ere* = *con* + *reg'ere), to remove faults;* direct' (-ion, -or, -ory); erect'; insurrec'tion; resurrec'tion.

Re'gal (Lat. n. *rex, re'gis,* a king); rega'lia; reg'icide (Lat. v. *cæd'ere,* to kill); reg'ular (Lat. n. *reg'ula,* a rule); reg'ulate; realm (Old Fr. *realme,* from Lat. adj. *rega'lis,* royal); reign (Fr. n. *règne* = Lat. *reg'num);* corrigen'da (sing. *corrigen'dum), things to be corrected;* dress (Fr. v. *dresser* = Lat *dirig'ere*); address' (Fr. v. *adresser,* to direct); redress' (Fr. v. *redresser* = Lat. *re* + *dirig'ere), to rectify, to repair;* source (Fr. n. *source,* from Lat. *sur'gere,* to spring up); surge; insur'gent (Lat. v. *insur'gere*).

174. RI'VUS, a river.

riv: ri'val (Lat. n. *riva'lis,* one who used a brook in common with another); ri'valry; outri'val; riv'ulet (Lat. n. *riv'ulus,* diminutive of *ri'vus*); derive' (literally, to receive as from a source); deriva'tion; deriv'ative.

175. ROGA'RE: ro'go, roga'tum, to ask.

rog: ar'rogant, *proud, overbearing*; ar'rogance; prorogue' (Fr. v. *proroger* = Lat. *proroga're*).

rogat: ab'rogate; *to repeal*; ar'rogate, *to assume*; arroga'tion; derog'atory, *detracting*; inter'rogate (-ion, -ive, -ory); prerog'ative (literally, that is asked before others for an opinion: hence, preference), *exclusive or peculiar right or privilege*; proroga'tion, *prolonga'tion*; superer'ogate (Lat. *super* + *eroga're*, to spend or pay out over and above), *to do more than is necessary*; supereroga'tion.

176. RUM'PERE: rum'po, rup'tum, to break.

rupt: rupt'ure, *to part violently*; abrupt' (-ly, -ness); bank'rupt (It. n. *banco*, a merchant's place of business); bank'ruptcy; corrupt' (-ible, -ion); disrup'tion; erup'tion; interrupt' (-ion); irrup'tion; irrup'tive.

177. SA'CER, sa'cri, holy.

sacr: sac'rament (Lat. n. *sacramen'tum*, an oath, a sacred thing); sa'cred (orignally, past p. of Old Eng. v. *sacre*, to consecrate); sac'rifice (Lat. v. *fac'ere*, to make); sac'rilege (literally, that steals—properly gathers, picks up, *leg'ere*—sacred things); sac'ristan (Low Lat. *sacrista'nus*), a church officer.

secr: (in comp.) con'secrate (-ion); des'ecrate (-ion); ex'ecrate (-ion); ex'ecrable; sacerdo'tal (Lat. n. *sacer'dos, sacerdo'tis*, priest), *pertaining to the priesthood.*

178. SA'LUS, salu'tis, health; Sal'vus, safe.

salut: sal'utary, *promoting health*; salu'tatory, *giving salutation*; salute' (-ion).

salv: sal'vage, *reward for saving goods*; sal'vo, *a volley*; salva'tion.

Safe (through Old Fr. *salf* or *sauf*); safe'ty; save; sav'ior salu'brious (Lat. adj. *salu'bris*, health-giving); salu'brity.

179. SCAN'DERE: scan'do (in comp. scen'do), scan'dum (in comp. scen'sum), to climb.

scend: ascend' (-ant, -ency); descend' (-ant); condescend' (-ing); transcend' (-ent); transcendental.

scens: ascen'sion; ascent'; condescen'sion.

180. SCRIB'ERE: scri'bo, scrip'tum, to write.

scrib: ascribe', *to impute to*; circumscribe', *to draw a line around, to limit*; describe'; inscribe'; prescribe', *to order or appoint*; pro-scribe' (literally, to write forth), *to interdict*; subscribe'; superscribe'; transcribe'.

script: script, *type in imitation of handwriting*; script'ure; ascrip'tion; con'script, *one taken by lot and enrolled for military service*; conscrip'tion; descrip'tion; inscrip'tion; man'uscript (see *manus*); post'script; prescrip'tion; proscription; subscription; superscrip'tion; tran'script.

Scribe (Fr. n. *scribe*); scrib'ble; escritoire'.

181. SECA'RE: se'co, sec'tum, to cut.

sec: se'cant (Lat. pres. p. *se'cans, secan'tis*), *a line that cuts another*.

sect: sect (literally, a body of persons separated from others by peculiar doctrines); secta'rian (-ism); sec'tion (-al); bisect' (Lat. *bis*, two); dissect' (-ion); in'sect (literally, an animal whose body is apparently cut in the middle); insectiv'orous (Lat. v. *vora're*, to feed); intersect' (-ion); venesec'tion (Lat. n. *vena*, a vein).

Seg'ment (Lat. n. *segmen'tum*), *a part cut off*.

182. SEDE'RE: se'deo (in comp. se'do), ses'sum, to sit.

sed: sed'entary (Lat. adj. *sedenta'rius*, accustomed to sit); sed'iment (Lat. n. *sedimen'tum*, a settling or sinking down); sedimen'tary; sed'ulous (Lat. adj. *sed'ulus*, sitting close to an employment); supersede'.

sid: assid'uous; assidu'ity; insid'ious (literally, sitting in wait against); preside' (literally, to sit before or over); pres'ident; presidence; reside' (-ence); res'idue; resid'uary; subside'; subsidiary.

sess: ses'sion (-al); assess' (literally, to sit by or near a person or thing); assess'ment; assess'or; possess' (Lat. v. *possid'ere, posses'sum*, to sit upon: hence, to occupy in person, to have or hold); posses'sion; possess'or; posses'sive; prepossess', *to take possession of beforehand, to prejudice*.

183. SENTI'RE: sen'tio, sen'sum, to feel, to think.

sent: scent (Old English *sent*), *odor*; sen'tence (Lat. n. *senten'tia*); senten'tious (Lat. adj. *sententio'sus*, full of thought); sentiment (Fr. n. *sentiment*); sentimen'tal; assent', *to agree to*; consent' (literally, to think or feel together), *to acquiesce, to permit*; dissent' (-er); dissen'tient; presen'timent; resent' (literally, to feel back), *to take ill*; resent'ment.

sens: sense (-less, -ation, -ible, -itive); insen'sate; non'sense; sen'sual (Lat. adj. *sensua'lis*); sen'sualist; sen'suous.

184. SE'QUI: se'quor, secu'tus, to follow.

sequ: se'quence, *order of succession*; consequent; con'sequence; consequential; ob'sequies, *formal rites*; obse'quious (literally, following in the way of another), *meanly condescending*; sub'sequent (-ly).

secut: consec'utive; persecute (-ion, -or); pros'ecute (-ion).

Se'quel (Lat. n. *seque'la*, that which follows); sue (Old Fr. v. *suire*, New Fr. *suivre* = *se'qui*), *to follow at law*; suit; suit'able; suit'or; suite (Fr. n. *suite*), *a train or set*; ensue' (Fr. v. *ensuivre*, to follow, to result from); pursue' (Fr. v. *poursuivre*, to follow hard, to chase); pursu'ance; pursu'ant; pursuit'; pur'suivant, *a state messenger*; ex'ecute (Fr. v. *executer* = Lat. *ex'sequi*); execu'tion; exec'utor; exec'utrix.

185. SERVA'RE: ser'vo, serva'tum, to save, to keep, to bind.

serv: conserve'; observe' (-able, -ance); preserve' (-er); reserve'; unreserved'.

servat: conserv'ative; conserv'atory; observ'ation; observ'atory; preserva'tion; preserv'ative; reserva'tion.

Res'ervoir (Fr. n. *réservoir* = Lat. *reservato'rium*, a place where anything is kept in store).

EXERCISE.

The puzzle is *complicated* and *displays* much *ingenuity* on the *part* of the inventor. A *reply* may be *explicit* without showing *duplicity*. It was urged that the *election* of *delegates* be *postponed*. The *portmanteau* containing *important* papers was left at the *merchant's office*. An *impostor* is sure to show *opposition* to the course of *justice*. Coleridge holds that it is *possible* to *apprehend* a truth without *comprehending* it. The *bankrupt* was so *arrogant* that his *creditors* were not *disposed* to be lenient with him. Most of the questions *proposed* by the *rector* were answered in the *negative*. What is the origin of the word *derivation*? The *region* is *described* as healthful. The *manuscript* was *transcribed* and *subscribed* by the *author*. It is *salutary* to be *rivals* in all worthy *ambitions*.

186. SIG'NUM, a sign.

sign: sign; sig'nal (-ize); sig'net; sig'nify; signif'icant; signif'icance; significa'tion; assign' (Lat. v. *assigna're, to designate*); assignee'; consign' (Lat. v. *consigna're, to seal*) *to intrust to another*; consign'ment; coun'tersign, *to sign what has already been signed by another*; design', *to plan*; design'er; des'ignate, *to name, to point out*; designa'tion; en'sign, *the officer who carries the flag of a regiment*; insig'nia, *badges of office*; resign' (-ation); sig'nature (Lat. n. *signatu'ra*, a sign or stamp).

187. SIM'ILIS, like.

simil: sim'ilar (-ity); sim'i-le, *a formal likening or comparison*; simil'itude; verisimil'itude (Lat. adj. *ve'rus*, true); dissim'ilar; assim'ilate; fac-sim'ile (Lat. v. *fac'ere*, to make), an exact copy; sim'ulate (Lat. v. *simula're, simula'tum*, to make like).

Dissimula'tion (Lat. v. *dissimula're, dissimula'tum*, to feign); dissem'ble (Fr. v. *dissembler* = Lat. *dissimula're*); resem'ble (Fr. v. *ressembler*).

188. SIS'TERE: sisto, sta'tum, to cause to stand, to stand.

sist: assist' (-ance, -ant); consist' (-ent, -ency); desist'; exist' (for ex-sist), *to stand out*: hence, *to be, to live*; exist'ence; co-exist'; pre-exist'; insist', *to stand upon, to urge firmly*; persist' (-ent, -ence); resist' (-ance, -ible); subsist (-ence).

189. SOL'VERE: sol'vo, solu'tum, to loosen.

solv: solve (-able, -ent, -ency); absolve'; dissolve'; resolve'.

solut: solu'tion; ab'solute (-ion); dis'solute (-ion); res'olute (-ion).

Sol'uble (Lat. adj. *solu'bilis*); solubil'ity.

190. SPEC'ERE or SPIC'ERE: Spe'cio or spi'cio, spec'tum, to behold; Spe'cies, a kind.

spic: aus'pices (literally, omens drawn from the inspection of birds); auspi'cious; conspic'uous (Lat. adj. *conspic'uus*, wholly visible); conspicu'ity;

des'picable (Lat. *despicab'ilis*, deserving to be despised); perspic'uous (Lat. adj. *perspic'uus*, that may be seen through); perspicu'ity; suspi'cion; suspi'cious.

spect: as'pect; cir'cumspect (-ion); expect' (-ant, -ation); inspect' (-ion, -or); perspec'tive; pros'pect (-ive); prospec'tus (Lat. n. *prospec'tus*, a view forward); respect' (literally, to look again: hence, to esteem or regard); respect'able; respect'ful; re'tro-spect (-ive); suspect'.

species: spe'cies; spe'cial (-ist, -ity, -ize); spe'cie; spec'ify (-ic, -ication); spe'cious, *showy*.

Spec'imen (Lat. n. *spec'imen*, a sample); spec'tacle (Lat. n. *spectac'ulum*, anything presented to view); specta'tor (Lat. n. *specta'tor*, a beholder); spec'ter (Lat. n. *spec'trum*, an image); spec'tral; spec'trum (pl. spec'tra), *an image*; spec'troscope (Gr. v. *skopein*, to view), *an instrument for analysing light*; spec'ulate (Lat. n. *spec'ula*, a lookout), *to contemplate, to traffic for great profit*; specula'tion; spec'ulative.

191. SPIRA'RE: spi'ro, spira'tum, to breathe; Spir'itus, breath, spirit.

spir: spir'acle, *a breathing pore*; aspire' (-ant); conspire' (-acy); expire'; expir'ing; inspire'; perspire'; respire'; transpire'.

spirat: aspira'tion; as'pirate; conspir'ator; inspira'tion; perspira'tion; respira'tion; respir'atory.

spiritus: spir'it; spir'itual (-ity); spir'ituous.

Sprightly (spright, a contraction of spirit); sprite (a contraction of spirit).

192. SPONDE'RE: spon'deo, spon'sum, to promise.

spond: correspond', *to answer one to another*; correspond'ence; correspond'ent; despond' (literally, to promise away: hence, to give up, to despond); despond'ency; respond'.

spons: spon'sor, *a surety*; response' (-ible, -ibility, -ive); irrespon'sible.

Spouse (Old Fr. n. *espous, espouse* = Lat. *spon'sus, spon'sa*); espouse' (Old Fr. v. *espouser* = Lat. *sponsa're*, to betroth, from *spondere*).

193. STA'RE: sto, sta'tum (in comp. sti'tum, to stand; pres. part. stans, stan'tis, standing); SIS'TERE: sis'to, sta'tum, to cause to stand; STATU'ERE: stat'uo, statu'tum, to station, to fix, to place.

stant: cir'cumstance (from part. *circumstans', circumstan'tis*, through Lat. n. *circumstan'tia*, Fr. *circonstance*), *the condition of things surrounding or attending an event*; circumstan'tial; circumstan'tiate; con'stant; con'stancy; dis'tant (literally, standing asunder: hence, remote, reserved); dis'tance; ex'tant; in'stant; instanta'neous; transubstan'tiate, *to change to another substance*.

stat: state; sta'tion (-ary, -er, -ery); state'ly; state'ment; states'man; stat'ue (-ary); stat'ure.

stit: supersti'tion (literally, a standing over, as if awe-struck); supersti'tious.

statut: stat'ute (-ory).

stitu: con'stitute (literally, to set or station together: hence, to establish, to make); constitu'tion (-al); constituent; constit'uency; des'titute (literally, put from or away: hence, forsaken, in want of); in'stitute (literally, to place into: hence, to found, to commence); restitu'tion; sub'stitute (-ion).

Sta'ble; (Lat. adj. *stab'ilis*, standing firmly); stab'lish; estab'lish (-ment); stay, literally, *to keep standing*; ar'mistice (Lat. n. *ar'ma*, arms), *a temporary stand-still of war*; arrest' (Old Fr. *arrester* = Lat. *ad + restare*, to stay back, to remain); contrast' (Lat. *contra + sta're*, to stand against); inter'stice; ob'stacle; ob'stinate; sol'stice (Lat. n. *sol*, the sun).

194. STRIN'GERE: strin'go, stric'tum, to bind; to draw tight.

string: strin'gent; astrin'gent; astrin'gency.

strict: strict (-ness, -ure); dis'trict, *a defined portion of a country*; restrict' (-ion).

Strain (Old Fr. *straindre* = Lat. *strin'gere*); constrain'; dis-train'; restrain'; restraint'.

195. STRU'ERE: stru'o, struc'tum, to build, to place in order.

struct: struct'ure; construct' (-ion, -ive); destruct'ible; destruc'tion; instruct' (-ion,-ive,-or); obstruct'(-ion); superstruct'ure.

Con'strue; destroy'; in'strument (Lat. n. *instrumen'tum*); instrumental'ity.

196. SU'MERE: su'mo, sump'tum, to take; Sump'tus, cost, expense.

sum: assume'; consume' (-er); presume'; resume'.

sumpt: sumpt'uous (Lat. adj. *sumptuo'sus*, expensive); sumpt'uary, *relating to expense*; assumption; consumption; consump'tive; presump'tion; presump'tive; presump'tuous.

197. TAN'GERE: tan'go, tac'tum, to touch.

tang: tan'gent, *a straight line which touches a circle or curve*; tan'gible.

tact: tact, *peculiar faculty or skill*; con'tact; intact'.

Attain' (Fr. v. *attaindre*, to reach); attain'able; conta'gion, *communication of disease by contact or touch*; contam'inate, *to defile, to infect*; contig'uous; contin'gent.

TEMPUS. (See page 48.)

198. TEN'DERE: ten'do, ten'sum or ten'tum, to stretch.

tend: tend, *to aim at, take care of*; tend'ency; attend' (-ance, -ant); contend'; distend'; extend'; intend' (literally, to stretch to), *to purpose, to design*; portend' (literally, to stretch forward), *to presage, to betoken*; pretend' (literally, to stretch forth), *to affect, feel*; subtend', *to extend under*; superintend' (-ence, -ent).

tens: tense (adj.), *stretched*; ten'sion; intense' (-ify); osten'sible (Lat. v. *osten'dere*, to stretch out or spread before one), *apparent*; pretense'.

tent: tent, literally, *a shelter of stretched canvas*; tentac'ula, *the feelers of certain animals*; atten'tion; atten'tive; conten'tion; conten'tious; extent'; intent' (-ion); ostenta'tion; ostenta'tious; por'tent, *an ill omen*.

199. TENE'RE: ten'eo, ten'tum, to hold; French Tenir (radical tain), to hold.

ten: ten'able; ten'ant, *one who holds property under another*; ten'antry; ten'ement; ten'et (Lat. *tenet*, literally, "he holds"), *a doctrine held as true*; ten'ure.

tin (in compos.): ab'stinent; ab'stinence; continent; incon'tinent; per'tinent; imper'tinent.

tent: content' (-ment); contents'; discontent'; deten'tion; reten'tion; reten'tive; sus'tenance.

tain: abstain'; appertain'; contain'; detain'; entertain' (-ment); pertain'; retain' (-er); sustain'.

Tena'cious (Lat. adj. *te'nax, tena'cis*, holding firmly); tenac'ity; appur'tenance, *that which belongs to something else*; contin'ue (Fr. v. *continuer* = Lat. *contine're*); contin'ual; contin'uance; continua'tion; continu'ity; discontin'ue; coun'tenance (literally, the contents of a body: hence, of a face); lieuten'ant (Fr. n. *lieu*, a place); maintain' (Fr. n. *main*, the hand), literally, *to hold by the hand*: hence, *to support, to uphold*; main'tenance; pertina'cious; pertinac'ity; ret'inue, *a train of attendants*.

200. TER'RA, the earth.

terr: ter'race (Fr. n. *terrasse*); terra'queous (Lat. n. *a'qua*, water); terres'trial; ter'ritory (-al); ter'rier, *a small dog that goes into the ground after burrowing animals*; Mediterra'nean (Lat. n. *me'dius*, middle); subterra'nean.

Inter, *to put in the earth, to bury*; inter'ment; disinter'.

201. TES'TIS, a witness.

test: tes'tify; attest' (-ation); contest'; detest' (-able); protest' (-ation, -ant); prot'estantism.

Tes'tament (Lat. n. *testamen'tum*, a will); testamen'tary; testa'tor; tes'timony (-al); intes'tate, *not having left a will.*

202. TOR'QUERE: tor'queo, tor'tum, to twist.

tort: tort'ure; contort' (-ion); distort' (-ion); extort' (-ion, -ionate); retort'.

Tor'tuous (Lat. adj. *tortuo'sus*, very twisted); tortuos'ity; torment' (Lat. n. *tormen'tum*, extreme pain).

203. TRA'HERE: tra'ho, trac'tum, to draw; Fr. Trair, past part. Trait.

tract: tract (-able, -ile, -ion); ab'stract (-ion); attract' (-ion, -ive); contract' (-ile, -or); detract'; distract'; extract' (-ion, -or); protract'; retract' (-ion); subtract' (-ion).

Trace (Fr. n. *trace*); track (Old Fr. n. *trac*); train; trait; treat (-ise, -ment, -y).

204. TRIBU'ERE: trib'uo, tribu'tum, to allot, to give.

tribut: trib'ute (-ary); attrib'ute; contribute (-ion); distrib'ute (-ion, -ive); retribu'tion; retrib'utive.

205. TRU'DERE: tru'do, tru'sum, to thrust.

trud: detrude', *to thrust down;* extrude'; intrude' (-er); obtrude'; protrude'.

trus: abstruse' (literally, thrust away: hence, difficult to be understood); intru'sion; intru'sive; obtru'sive; protru'sion.

206. TU'ERE: tu'eor, tu'itus or tu'tus, to watch.

tuit: tui'tion, *instruction;* intui'tion, *the act or power of the mind by which it at once perceives the truth of a thing without argument;* intu'itive.

tut: tu'tor; tuto'rial; tu'torage.

207. UN'DA, a wave.

und: abun'dance, literally, condition of overflowing—(*abunda're*, to overflow); abun'dant; superabundant; inun'date (-ion); redun'dant (literally, running back or over: hence, exceeding what is necessary); redundance; redun'dancy.

Un'dulate (Lat. n. *un'dula*, a little wave); undula'tion; un'dulatory; abound'; superabound'; redound' (Old Fr. v. *redonder* = Lat. *redunda're*, to roll back as a wave or flood).

208. U'TI: u'tor, u'sus, to use.

ut: uten'sil (Lat. n. *uten'sile*, something that may be used); util'ity (Lat. n. *util'itas*, usefulness); u'tilize.

us: use (-able, -age, -ful, -less); us'ual (Lat. adj. *usua'lis*, of frequent use); u'sury, *illegal interest paid for the use of money*; u'surer; abuse' (-ive); disabuse'.

209. VAD'ERE: va'do, va'sum, to go.

vad: evade'; invade'; pervade'.

vas: eva'sion; inva'sion; perva'sive.

210. VALE'RE: valeo, vali'tum, to be strong, to be of value; Val'idus, strong; Va'le, farewell.

val: valedic'tory, *bidding farewell*; valetudina'rian (Lat. n. *valetu'do*, state of health), *a person in ill-health*; val'iant, *brave, heroic*; val'or (-ous); val'ue (-able, -ation, -ator); convales'cent, *regaining health*; equiv'alent (Lat. adj. *e'quus*, equal); prev'alent, *very common or general*; prevalence.

vail: (Fr. radical): avail' (-able); prevail'.

valid: val'id; valid'ity; in'valid.

211. VENI'RE: ve'nio, ven'tum, to come, to go.

vent: vent'ure, literally, *something gone upon*; vent'uresome; ad'vent; adventi'tious, *accidental, casual*; advent'ure (-ous); circumvent'; contraven'tion; con'vent, *a monastery, a nunnery*; conven'ticle, *a place of assembly*; conven'tion (-al); event'(-ful); event'ual; invent' (literally, *to come upon*), *to find out, to contrive*; inven'tion; invent'ive; invent'or; interven'tion; peradvent'ure; prevent' (-ion, -ive).

Av'enue (Fr. n. *avenue*, an approach to); contravene'; convene'; conven'ient (Lat. pres. part, *conve'niens, convenien'tis*, literally, coming together), *suitable*; conven'ience; cov'enant *an agreement between two parties*; intervene'; rev'enue; supervene', *to come upon, to happen*.

212. VER'BUM, a word.

verb: verb (-al, -ally, -ose, -osity); ad'verb; prov'erb.

Verba'tim (Lat. adv. *verba'tim*, word for word); ver'biage (Fr. n. *verbiage*, wordiness).

213. VER'TERE: ver'to, ver'sum, to turn.

vert: advert'; inadver'tent (literally, not turning the mind to), *heedless*; ad'vertise, *to turn public attention to*; adver'tisement; animadvert' (Lat. n. *an'imus*, the mind), *to turn the mind to, to censure*; avert'; controvert', *to oppose*; convert', *to change into another form or state*; divert'; invert', literally, *to turn the outside in*; pervert', *to turn from the true purpose*; retrovert'; revert'; subvert'.

vers: adverse' (-ary, -ity); animadver'sion; anniver'sary, *the yearly* (Lat. n. *an'nus*, a year) *celebration of an event*; averse', *having a dislike to*; aver'sion; con'troversy; converse' (-ant, -ation); conver'sion; diverse' (-ify, -ion, -ity); ob'verse; perverse' (-ity); retrover'sion; reverse' (-al, -ion); subver'sion; subversive; tergiversa'tion (Lat. n. *ter'gum*, the back), *a subterfuge*; transverse', *lying or being across*; u'niverse (Lat. adj. *u'nus*, one), *the system* *of created things*; univer'sal (-ist); univer'sity, *a universal school in which are taught all branches of learning.*

Verse (Lat. n. *ver'sus*, a furrow), *a line in poetry*; ver'sify; versifica'tion; ver'sion, *that which is turned from one language into another, a statement*; ver'satile (Lat. adj. *versat'ilis*, turning with ease); vertex (pl. ver'tices), *the summit*; vertical; vertebra (pl. ver'tebræ); ver'tebrate; ver'tigo; vor'tex (Lat. n. *vor'tex*, a whirlpool); divorce' (Fr. n. *divorce), a separation.*

214. VE'RUS, true; Ve'rax, vera'cis, veracious.

ver: ver'dict (Lat. n. *dic'tum*, a saying), *the decision of a jury*; ver'ify, *to prove to be true*; verifica'tion; ver'ity (Lat. n. *ver'itas*, truth); ver'itable; verisim'ilar, *truth-like*; verisimil'itude; aver', *to declare truer*; aver'ment; ver'ily; ver'y.

verac: v'era'cious; verac'ity.

215. VI'A, a way.

via: vi'aduct (Lat. v. *du'cere, duc'tum*, to lead); viat'icum (Lat. n. *viat'icum*, literally, traveling money), *the sacrament administered to a dying person*; de'viate (-ion); de'vious; ob'viate, *to meet in the way, to remove*; ob'vious; per'vious, *affording a passage through*; imper'vious.

Voy'age (Fr. n. *voyage*); convoy', *to escort*; en'voy (Fr. v. *envoyer*, to send), *one sent on a special mission*; triv'ial (Lat. n. *triv'ium*, a cross road), *trifling*; trivial'ity.

216. VIDE'RE: vi'deo, vi'sum, to see.

vid: ev'ident, *clearly seen;* ev'idence; invid'ious, literally, *looking against*: hence, *likely to provoke envy*; provide', *to look out for, to supply*; prov'idence; prov'ident.

vis: vis'ible; vis'ion (-ary); advise'; advis'able, *expedient*; im'provise, *to compose and recite without premeditation*; provis'ion; revise' (-al, -ion); supervis'ion; supervis'or.

View (Fr. v. *voir*, to see, *vu*, seen); review'; in'terview; vis'age (Fr. n. *visage*, the countenance); vis'it (-ant, -or, -ation); vis'or, *part of a helmet perforated to see through;* vis'ta (It. n. *vista*, sight), *a prospect as seen through an avenue of trees* ; advice'; en'vy (Fr. n. *envie* = Lat. *invid'ia*, from *invide're*, to see against); in'voice (It. n. *avviso*, notice), *a priced list of goods;* peruse' (Lat. v. *pervide're, pervi'sum*, to look through); provi'so, *a stipulation;* pru'dent (Lat. adj. *pru'dens* from *prov'idens*); pru'dence; purvey', *to look out for in the way of buying provisions;* purvey'or; survey' (-or).

217. VIN'CERE: vin'co, vic'tum, to conquer.

vinc: vin'cible; invin'cible; convince'; evince', *to show clearly*

vict: vic'tor; vic'tory (-ous); convict', *to prove guilty of crime;* evict', *to dispossess;* evic'tion.

Vanquish (Fr. v. *vaincre, vaincu* = Lat. *vin'cere*); prov'ince (Fr. n. *province* = Lat. *provin'cia*, literally, a conquered country).

218. VOCA'RE: vo'co, voca'tum, to call; Vox, vo'cis, the voice.

vocat: voca'tion, literally, *calling, occupation;* voc'ative, *the case of a noun in which the subject is called, or addressed;* ad'vocate *to plead for;* convoca'tion, *an assembly, a meeting;* equivocate (Lat. adj. *e'quus*, equal), *to use words of doubtful meaning;* equivoca'tion; evoca'tion, *act of calling forth;* invoca'tion; provoca'tion; provo'cative; revoca'tion.

voc: vo'cable (Lat. n. *vocab'ulum*, that which is sounded with the voice), *a word;* vocab'ulary; vo'cal (-ist, -ize); vociferate, *to cry with a loud voice;* ad'vocacy, *a pleading for, a defense;* irrev'ocable.

Voice (Fr. n. *voix* = Lat. *vox), sound uttered by the mouth;* vouch, *to call out, or affirm strongly;* vow'el (Fr. n. *vouelle*, a voice-sound); advow'son, *right of perpetual calling to a benefice;* convoke', *to call together;* evoke'; invoke'; revoke'.

219. VOL'VERE: vol'vo, volu'tum, to roll.

volv: circumvolve'; convolve', *to roll together*; devolve'; evolve'; involve'; revolve' (-ion, -ionist).

volut: circumvolu'tion; evolu'tion; revolution (-ary, -ist, -ize).

Vol'ume (Lat. n. *volu'men*, a roll, or inscribed parchment sheet rolled up), *a single book*; volute', *a kind of rolled or spiral scroll*; vol'uble, literally, *rolling easily*: hence, *having great fluency of speech*; convol'vulus, *a genus of twining plants*; revolt'.

220. VUL'GUS, the common people.

vulg: vul'gar; vul'garism; vulgar'ity; vul'gate, *a Latin version of the Scriptures.*

Divulge', *to make known something before kept secret*; divulge'ment; promulgate (-ion).

PART III.—THE GREEK ELEMENT.

I.—GREEK PREFIXES.

Prefix.	Signification.	Example.	Definition
a- an-	= *without;* *not*	a-pathy an-omalous	state of being *without* feeling. *not* similar.
amphi-	= *around;* *both*	amphi-theater amphi-bious	place for seeing all *around.* living in *both* land and water.
ana-	= *back,* *throughout*	ana-logy ana-lysis	reasoning *back.* loosening *throughout.*
anti- ant-	= *against;* *opposite*	anti-pathy ant-arctic	a feeling *against.* *opposite* the Arctic.
apo- ap-	= *away;* *out*	apo-stle ap-helion	one sent *out.* *away* from the sun.
cata- cat-	= *down* or *against*	cata-ract cat-arrh	a rushing *down.* a flowing *down.*

dia-	= *through* or *across*	dia-meter dia-logue	measure *through* the center. speaking *across* (from one another).
dis- di-	= *two, double*	dis-syllable di-lemma	word of *two* syllables. a *double* assumption.
dys-	= *ill*	dys-pepsia	*ill* digestion.
ec- ex-	= *out of*	ec-centric ex-odies	*out of* the center. an *outgoing*.

Note—**ex-** is used before a root beginning with a vowel.

en- em-	= *in* or *on*	en-ergy em-phasis	power *in* one. stress *on*.
epi- ep-	= *upon; for*	epi-dermis ep-hemeral	skin *upon* skin. lasting *for* a day.

Note—**ep-** is used before a root beginning with a vowel or a *h* aspirate

eu- ev-	= *well* or *good*	eu-phonic ev-angel	sounding *well*. *good* news.
hemi-	= *half*	hemi-sphere	*half* a sphere

hyper-	= *over* or *beyond*	hyper-critical hyper-borean	*over*-critical. *beyond* the North.
hypo-	= *under*	hypo-thesis	a placing *under* (= Lat. supposition.)
meta- met-	= *beyond*; *transference*	meta-physics met-onymy	science *beyond* physics. *transference* of name.
para- par-	= *by the side of*	par-helion	mock sun *by the side of* the real.
peri-	= around	peri-meter	the measure *around* anything.
pro-	= before	pro-gramme	something written *before*.
pros-	= to	pros-elyte	one coming *to* a new religion.
syn- sy- syl- sym-	*with* = or *together*	syn-thesis sy-stem syl-lable sym-pathy	placing *together*. part *with* part. letters taken *together*. feeling *together*.

NOTE.—The form **sy-** is used before *s*; **syl-** before *l*, **sym-** before *b*, *p* or *m*.

II.—GREEK ALPHABET.

A α	a	*Alpha.*
B β	b	*Beta.*
Γ γ	g	*Gamma.*
Δ δ	d	*Delta.*
E ε	e as in *met*	*Epsilon.*
Z ζ	z	*Zeta.*
H η	e as in *me*	*Eta.*
Θ θ	th	*Theta.*
I ι	i	*Iota*
K κ	k	*Kappa.*
Λ λ	l	*Lambda.*
M μ	m	*Mu.*
N ν	n	*Nu.*
Ξ ξ	x	*Xi.*
O o	o as in *not*	*Omicron.*
	p	*Pi*
Π π	r	*Rho.*
P ρ	s	*Sigma.*
Σ σ, ς final	t	*Tau.*
T τ	u, or y	*Upsilon.*
Y υ	ph	*Phi.*
Φ φ	ch	*Chi.*
X χ	ps	*Psi.*
Ψ ψ	o as in *no*	*Omega.*
Ω ω		

Pronunciation of Greek Words.

Gamma has always the hard sound of *g*, as in *give*.

Kappa is represented by *c* in English words, although in Greek it has but one sound, that of our *k*.

Upsilon is represented by *y* in English words; in Greek it has always the sound of *u* in mute.

Chi is represented in English by *ch* having the sound of *k*; as in *chronic*.

In Greek words, as in Latin, there are always as many syllables as there are vowels and diphthongs.

An inverted comma placed over a letter denotes that the sound of our *h* precedes that letter.

GREEK ROOTS AND ENGLISH DERIVATIVES.

DIVISION I.—PRINCIPAL GREEK ROOTS.

1. A'ER (αηρ), *the air.*

a'erate, *to combine with air; to mix with carbonic acid.*

a-e'rial, *belonging to the air.*

a'eriform, *having the form of air.*

a'erolite (Gr. n. *lith'os*, a stone), *a meteoric stone.*

a'eronaut (Gr. n. *nau'tēs*, a sailor), *a balloonist.*

aerosta'tion, *aerial navigation.*

air, *the atmosphere; a melody; the bearing of a person.*

air'y, *open to the air; gay, sprightly.*

2. AG'EIN (αγειν), *to lead.*

apago'ge, *a leading away; an indirect argument*

dem'agogue (Gr. n. *de'mos*, the people), *a misleader of the people.*

parago'ge (literally, a leading or extension beyond), *the addition of a letter or syllable to the end of a word.*

ped'agogue (Gr. n. *pais*, a child), *a schoolmaster; a pedantic person..*

syn'agogue, *a Jewish place of worship.*

3. A'GON (αγων), a contest.

ag'ony, *extreme pain.*

ag'onize, *to be in agony.*

antag'onism, *direct opposition.*

antag'onist, *or* **antagonis'tic**, *contending against.*

4. ANG'ELLEIN (αγγελλειν), *to bring tidings;* ANG'ELLOS (αγγελλος), *a messenger.*

an'gel, *a spiritual messenger.*

angel'ic, *relating to an angel.*

archan'gel (Gr. prefix *archi-*, chief), *an angel of the highest order.*

evan'gel (Gr. prefix *eu*, well), *good tidings; the gospel.*

evan'gelist, *one of the writers of the four gospels.*

5. AR'CHE (αρχη), *beginning, government, chief.*

an'archy, *want of government.*

ar'chitect (Gr. n. *tek'tōn*, workman), literally, *a chief builder, one who devises plans for buildings.*

ar'chives, *records.*

hep'tarchy (Gr. *hepta*, seven), *a sevenfold government.*

hi'erarchy (Gr. adj. *hi'eros*, sacred), *dominion in sacred things; a sacred body of rulers.*

mon'arch (Gr. adj. *mon'os*, alone), *one who rules alone, a sovereign.*

mon'archy, *government by one person, a kingdom.*

oligarchy (Gr. adj. *ol'igos*, few), *government by a few, an aristocracy.*

pa'triarch (Gr. n. *pat'ēr*, a father), *the father and ruler of a family.*

patriar'chal, *relating to patriarchs.*

6. AS'TRON (αστρον), *a star.*

as'terisk, *a mark like a star (*) used to refer to a note, and sometimes to mark an omission of words.*

as'teroid (Gr. adj. *ei'dos*, like), *one of the numerous small planets between Mars and Jupiter.*

as'tral, *belonging to the stars.*

astrol'ogy, *the pretended science of foretelling events by the stars.*

astron'omy (Gr. n. *nom'os*, a law), *the science that treats of the stars.*

astron'omer, *one skilled in astronomy.*

disas'ter, *calamity, misfortune.*

disas'trous, *unlucky; calamitous.*

7. AU'TOS (αυτος), *one's self.*

autobiog'raphy (Gr. n. *bi'os*, life, *graph'ein*, to write), *the life of a person written by himself.*

au'tocrat (Gr. n. *krat'os*, power), *an absolute ruler.*

autocrat'ic, *like an autocrat.*

au'tograph, *one's own handwriting.*

autom'aton (Gr. *mema'otes*, striving after), *a self-acting machine.*

authen'tic, *genuine, true.*

authentic'ity, *genuineness.*

8. BAL'LEIN (βαλλειν), *to throw or cast.*

em'blem, *a representation; a type.*

emblemat'ical, *containing an emblem.*

hyper'bole, *a figure of speech which represents things greater or less than they are.*

par'able, *a story which illustrates some fact or doctrine.*

parab'ola, *one of the conic sections.*

prob'lem, *a question proposed for solution.*

sym'bol, *a sign; a representation.*

symbolical, *representing by signs.*

9. BAP'TEIN (βαπτειν), *to wash, to dip.*

bap'tism, *a Christian sacrament, in the observance of which the individual is sprinkled with or immersed in water.*

baptize', *to sprinkle with or immerse in water.*

baptismal, *pertaining to baptism: as baptismal vows.*

bap'tist, *one who approves only of baptism by immersion.*

anabap'tist, *one who believes that only adults should be baptized.*

catabap'tist, *one opposed to baptism.*

pedobap'tism (Gr. *pais, paidos,* a child), *infant baptism.*

10. CHRON'OS (χρονος), time.

chron'ic, *lasting a long time; periodical.*

chron'icle, *a record of events in the order of time; a history recording facts in order of time.*

chronol'ogy, *the science of computing the dates of past events.*

chronom'eter (Gr. n. *me'tron,* a measure), *an instrument for measuring time.*

anach'ronism, *an error in computing time.*

syn'chronal, **syn'chronous**, *existing at the same time.*

11. GRAM'MA (γραμμα), *a letter*

gram'mar, *the science of language.*

gramma'rian, *one skilled in or who teaches grammar.*

grammat'ical, *according to the rules of grammar.*

an'agram, *the change of one word into another by transposing the letters.*

di'agram, *a writing or drawing made for illustration.*

ep'igram, *a short poem ending with a witty thought.*

mon'ogram (Gr. adj. *mon'os*, alone), *a character composed of several letters interwoven.*

pro'gramme, *order of any entertainment.*

tel'egram (Gr. *te'le*, at a distance), *a message sent by telegraph.*

12. GRAPH'EIN (γραφειν), *to write.*

graph'ic, *well delineated; giving vivid description.*

au'tograph. See *au'tos.*

biog'raphy (Gr. n. *bi'os*, life), *the history of a life.*

calig'raphy (Gr. adj. *kal'os*, beautiful), *beautiful writing.*

geog'raphy (Gr. n. *gē*, the earth), *a description of the earth.*

historiog'rapher (Gr. n. *histo'ria*, history), *one appointed to write history.*

hol'ograph (Gr. adj. *hol'os*, whole), *a deed or will wholly written by the grantor or testator.*

lexicog'rapher (Gr. n. *lex'icon*, a dictionary), *the compiler of a dictionary.*

lith'ograph (Gr. n. *lith'os*, a stone), *an impression of a drawing made on stone.*

lithog'raphy, *the art of writing on and taking impressions from stone.*

orthog'raphy (Gr. adj. *or'thos*, correct), *the correct spelling of words.*

pho'nograph (Gr. n. *pho'ne*, sound), *an instrument for the mechanical registration and reproduction of audible sounds.*

phonog'raphy, *a system of short hand; the art of constructing or of using the phonograph.*

photog'raphy (Gr. n. *phos, phot'os*, light), *the art of producing pictures by light.*

stenog'raphy (Gr. adj. *sten'os*, narrow), *the art of writing in short-hand.*

tel'egraph (Gr. *te'le*, at a distance), *an apparatus for conveying intelligence to a distance by means of electricity.*

topog'raphy (Gr. n. *top'os*, a place), *the description of a particular place.*

typography (Gr. n. *tu'pos*, a type), *the art or operation of printing.*

13. HOD'OS ('οδος), *a way.*

ep'isode, *an incidental story introduced into a poem or narrative.*

ex'odus, *departure from a place; the second book of the Old Testament.*

meth'od, *order, system, way, manner.*

Meth'odist, *the followers of John Wesley.* (The name has reference to the strictness of the rules of this sect of Christians).

pe'riod (Gr. n. *period'os*, a passage round), *the time in which anything is performed; a kind of sentence; a punctuation mark.*

syn'od, *a meeting of ecclesiastics.*

14. HU'DOR ('υδορ), *water.*

hy'dra, *a water-snake; a fabulous monster serpent slain by Hercules.*

hydran'gea, *a genus of plants remarkable for their absorption of water.*

hy'drant, *a water-plug.*

hydrau'lic (Gr. n. *au'los*, a pipe), *relating to the motion of water through pipes; worked by water.*

hydrau'lics, *the science which treats of fluids in motion.*

hydroceph'alus (Gr. n. *keph'ale*, the head), *dropsy of the head.*

hy'drogen (Gr. v. *gen'ein*, to beget), *a gas which with oxygen produces water.*

hydrog'raphy, *the art of maritime surveying and mapping.*

hydrop'athy (Gr. n. *path'os*, feeling), *the water-cure.*

hydropho'bia (Gr. n. *phob'os*, fear), literally, *dread of water; canine madness.*

hy'dropsy, *a collection of water in the body.* ("Dropsy" is a contraction of *hydropsy*).

hydrostat'ics, *the science which treats of fluids at rest.*

15. KRAT'OS (χρατος), *rule, government, strength.*

aristoc'racy (Gr. adj. *aris'tos*, best), *government by nobles.*

aris'tocrat, *one who favors aristocracy.*

au'tocrat. See *au'tos.*

democ'racy (Gr. n. *de'mos*, the people), *government by the people.*

dem'ocrat, *one who upholds democracy; in the United States, a member of the democratic party.*

theoc'racy, *government of a state by divine direction, as the ancient Jewish state.*

16. LOG'OS (λογος), *speech, ratio, description, science.*

log'ic, *the science and art of reasoning.*

logi'cian, *one skilled in logic.*

log'arithms (Gr. n. *arith'mos,* number), *a class of numbers that abridge arithmetical calculations.*

anal'ogy, *a resemblance of ratios.*

ap'ologue, *a moral fable.*

apol'ogy, *a defense, an excuse.*

cat'alogue, *a list of names in order.*

chronol'ogy. (See *chronos.*)

conchol'ogy (Gr. n. *kon'chos,* a shell), *the science of shells.*

dec'alogue (Gr. *dek'a,* ten), *the ten commandments.*

doxol'ogy (Gr. n. *doxa,* glory), *a hymn expressing glory to God.*

ec'logue, *a pastoral poem.*

entomol'ogy (Gr. n. *ento'ma,* insects, and v. *tem'nein,* to cut), *the natural history of insects.*

ep'ilogue, *a short poem or speech at the end of a play.*

etymol'ogy (Gr. *et'umon,* true source), *a part of grammar; the science of the derivation of words.*

eu'logy, *praise, commendation.*

geneal'ogy (Gr. n. *gen'os,* birth), *history of the descent of families.*

geol'ogy (Gr. n. *gē,* the earth), *the science which treats of the internal structure of the earth.*

mineral'ogy, *the science of minerals.*

mythol'ogy (Gr. n. *mu'thos*, a fable), *a system or science of fables.*

ornithol'ogy (Gr. n. *or'nis, or'nithos*, a bird), *the natural history of birds.*

pathol'ogy (Gr. n. *path'os*, suffering), *that part of medicine which treats of the causes and nature of diseases.*

philol'ogy (Gr. *phil'os*, loving, fond of), *the science which treats of languages.*

phrenol'ogy (Gr. n. *phrén*, the mind), *the art of reading the mind from the form of the skull.*

physiol'ogy (Gr. n. *phu'sis*, nature), *the science which treats of the organism of plants and animals.*

pro'logue, *verses recited as introductory to a play.*

psychol'ogy (Gr. n. *psu'che*, the soul), *mental philosophy; doctrine of man's spiritual nature.*

syl'logism, *a form of reasoning consisting of three propositions.*

tautol'ogy (Gr. *tau'to*, the same), *a repetition of the same idea in different words.*

technol'ogy (Gr. n. *tech'ne*, art), *a description of the arts.*

theol'ogy. See *theos.*

toxicol'ogy (Gr. n. *tox'icon*, poison) *the science which treats of poisons and their effects.*

zool'ogy (Gr. n. *zo'on*, an animal), *that part of natural history which treats of animals.*

17. MET'RON (μετρον) *a measure.*

me'ter, *arrangement of poetical feet; a measure of length.*

met'ric, *denoting measurement.*

met'rical, *pertaining to meter.*

anemom'eter (Gr. n. *an'emos*, the wind), *an instrument measuring the force and velocity of the wind.*

barom'eter (Gr. n. *ba'ros*, weight), *an instrument that indicates changes in the weather.*

diam'eter, *measure through anything.*

geom'etry (Gr. n. *ge*, the earth), *a branch of mathematics.*

hexam'eter (Gr. *hex*, six), *a line of six poetic feet.*

hydrom'eter (Gr. n. *hu'dor*, water), *an instrument for determining the specific gravities of liquids.*

hygrom'eter (Gr. adj. *hu'gros*, wet), *an instrument for measuring the degree of moisture of the atmosphere.*

pentam'eter (Gr. *pen'te*, five), *a line of five poetic feet.*

perim'eter, *the external boundary of a body or figure.*

sym'metry, *the proportion or harmony of parts.*

thermom'eter (Gr. adj. *ther'mos*, warm), *an instrument for measuring the heat of bodies.*

trigonom'etry (Gr. n. *trigo'non*, a triangle), *a branch of mathematics.*

18. MON'OS (μονος), *sole, alone.*

mon'achism, *the condition of monks; a monastic life.*

mon'ad, *something ultimate and indivisible.*

mon'astery, *a house of religious retirement.*

monk (Gr. n. *mon'achos*), *a religious recluse.*

monog'amy (Gr. n. *gam'os*, **marriage**), *the marriage of one wife only.*

mon'ologue (Gr. n. *log'os*), *a speech uttered by a person alone.*

monoma'nia (Gr. n. *ma'nia*, madness), *madness confined to one subject.*

monop'oly (Gr. v. pol'ein, to sell), *the sole power of selling anything.*

monosyl'lable, *a word of one syllable.*

mon'otheism (Gr. n. *the'os*, God), *the belief in the existence of only one God.*

mon'otone, *uniformity of tone.*

monot'ony, *sameness of sound; want of variety.*

19. O'DE (ωδε), *a song.*

ode, *a lyric poem.*

mel'ody (Gr. n. *mel'os*, a song), *an agreeable succession of musical sounds.*

par'ody, *the alteration of the works of an author to another subject.*

pros'ody, *the study of versification.*

psal'mody, *the practice of singing psalms.*

trag'edy (Gr. n. *trag'os*, a goat[9]), *a dramatic representation of a sad or calamitous event.*

EXERCISE.

The *periods* of *astronomy* go far beyond any *chronology*. The *phonograph* and the *telegraph* are both American inventions. By the aid of a *diagram* the *problem* was readily solved. Dr. Holmes, the *Autocrat* of the Breakfast Table, has written many *parodies*. In the struggle between *monarchy* and *democracy* Mexico has often been in a state of *anarchy*. His *antagonist* suffered great *agony* from the *disaster* that occurred. The *eulogy* pronounced on the great *zoölogist* Agassiz was well deserved. What is the *etymological* distinction between *geography* and *geology*? The *aeronaut* took with him a *barometer*, a *thermometer*, and a *chronometer*. I owe you an *apology* for not better knowing your *genealogy*. *Typography* has been well called "the art preservative of all the arts." Who is called the great American *lexicographer*? *Tautology* is to be avoided by all who make any pretence to *grammar*. One may be a *democrat* without being a *demagogue.* You cannot be an *architect* without knowing *geometry. Zoology* shows that there is great *symmetry* in the structure of animals. The pretensions of *astrology* are now dissipated into thin *air.* Many persons skilled in *physiology* do not believe in hydropathy. Longfellow's "Evangeline" is written in *hexameter,* and Milton's "Paradise Lost" in *pentameter.*

20. ON'OMA (ονομα), *a name.*

anon'ymous, *without a name.*

meton'ymy, *a rhetorical figure in which one word is put for another.*

on'omatopoe'ia, *the forming of words whose sound suggests the sense.*

paron'ymous, *of like derivation.*

patronym'ic (Gr. n. *pat'er,* a father), *a name derived from a parent or ancestor.*

pseu'donym (Gr. adj. *pseu'des,* false), *a fictitious name.*

syn'onym, *a word having the same meaning as another in the same language.*

21. PAN (παν, παντος), *all; whole.*

panace'a (Gr. v. *ak'eomai,* I cure), *a universal cure.*

pan'creas (Gr. n. *kre'as,* flesh), *a fleshy gland situated at the bottom of the stomach.*

pan'dect, *a treatise which combines the whole of any science.*

panegyr'ic (Gr. n. *ag'ora,* an assembly), *an oration in praise of some person or event.*

pan'oply (Gr. n. *hop'la,* armor), *a complete suit of armor.*

panora'ma (Gr. n. *hor'ama,* a sight or view), *a large picture gradually unrolled before an assembly.*

pan'theism (Gr. n. *the'os*, God), *the doctrine that nature is God.*

pan'theon, *a temple dedicated to all the gods.*

pan'tomime, *a scene or representation in dumb show.*

22. PA'THOS (παθος), *suffering, feeling.*

pathet'ic, *affecting the emotions.*

pathol'ogy, *the science of diseases.*

allop'athy, *a mode of medical practice.*

antip'athy, *dislike, aversion.*

ap'athy, *want of feeling.*

homeop'athy, *a mode of medical practice.*

hydrop'athy. See *hudor.*

sym'pathy, *fellow-feeling.*

23. PHIL'OS (φιλος), *a friend, a lover.*

Philadel'phia (Gr. n. *adel'phos*, a brother), literally, *the city of brotherly love.*

philanthropy (Gr. n. *anthro'pos*, a man), *love of mankind.*

philharmon'ic (Gr. n. *harmo'nia*, harmony), *loving harmony or music.*

philos'ophy (Gr. n. *sophi'a*, wisdom), *the general laws or principles belonging to any department of knowledge.*

philos'opher, *one versed in philosophy or science.*

philosoph'ic, **philosoph'ical**, *relating to philosophy.*

24. PHA'NEIN (φαινειν), *to cause to appear*; PHANTA'SIA (φαντασια), *an image, an idea.*

diaph'anous, *translucent.*

epiph'any, *the festival commemorative of the manifestation of Christ by the star of Bethlehem.*

fan'cy, *a pleasing image; a conceit or whim.*

fan'ciful, *full of fancy; abounding in wild images.*

fanta'sia, *a musical composition avowedly not governed by the ordinary musical rules.*

phan'tom, *a specter, an apparation.*

phase, *an appearance.*

phenom'enon, *anything presented to the senses by experiment or observation; an unusual appearance.*

syc'ophant (Gr. n. *sukon*, a fig, and, literally, an informer against stealers of figs), *a mean flatterer.*

25. PHO'NE (φωνη), *a sound.*

phonet'ic, **phon'ic**} *according to sound.*

eu'phony, *an agreeable sound of words.*

sym'phony, *harmony of mingled sounds; a musical composition for a full band of instruments.*

26. PHOS (φως, φωτος), *light.*

phos'phorus (Gr. v. *pherein*, to bear), *a substance resembling wax, highly inflammable, and luminous in the dark.*

phos'phate, *a salt of phosphoric acid.*

phosphores'cent, *luminous in the dark.*

phosphor'ic, *relating to or obtained from phosphorus.*

photog'raphy. See *graphein.*

27. PHU'SIS (φυσις), *nature.*

phys'ic, *medicines.*

phys'ical, *natural; material; relating to the body.*

physi'cian, *one skilled in the art of healing.*

phys'icist, *a student of nature.*

phys'ics, *natural philosophy.*

physiog'nomy (Gr. n. *gno'mon*, a judge), *the art of discerning the character of the mind from the features of the face; the particular cast of features or countenance.*

physiol'ogy. See *logos.*

metaphys'ics, literally, *after or beyond physics*; hence, *the science of mind.*

metaphysi'cian, *one versed in metaphysics.*

28. POL'IS (πολις), *a city.*

police', *the body of officers employed to secure the good order of a city.*

pol'icy, *the art or manner of governing a nation or conducting public affairs; prudence.*

pol'itic, *wise, expedient.*

polit'ical, *relating to politics.*

politi'cian, *one devoted to politics.*

pol'itics, *the art or science of government; struggle of parties.*

pol'ity, *the constitution of civil government.*

acrop'olis (Gr. adj. *ak'ros*, high), *a citadel.*

cosmop'olite (Gr. n. *kos'mos*, the world), *a citizen of the world.*

metrop'olis (Gr. n. *me'ter*, a mother), *the chief city of a country.*

necrop'olis (Gr. adj. *nek'ros*, dead), *a burial-place; a city of the dead.*

29. RHE'O ('ρεω), *I flow, I speak.*

rhet'oric, *the art of composition; the science of oratory.*

rhetori'cian, *one skilled in rhetoric.*

rheu'matism, *a disease of the limbs* (so called because the ancients supposed it to arise from a deflection of the humors).

res'in, *a gum which flows from certain trees.*

catarrh', *a discharge of fluid from the nose caused by cold in the head.*

diarrhoe'a, *purging.*

hem'orrhage (Gr. n. *haima*, blood), *a flowing of blood.*

30. SKOP'EIN (σκοπειν), *to see, to watch.*

scope, *space, aim, intention.*

bish'op (Gr. n. *epis'kopos*, overseer), *a clergyman who has charge of a diocese.*

epis'copacy, *church government by bishops.*

epis'copal, *relating to episcopacy.*

kalei'doscope (Gr. adj. *kal'os*, beautiful), *an optical instrument in which we see an endless variety of beautiful patterns by simple change of position.*

mi'croscope (Gr. adj. *mik'ros*, small), *an instrument for examining small objects.*

micros'copist, *one skilled in the use of the microscope.*

steth'oscope (Gr. n. *steth'os*, the breast), *an instrument for examining the state of the chest by sound.*

tel'escope (Gr. *te'le*, afar off), *an instrument for viewing objects far off.*

31. TAK'TOS (τακτος), *arranged;* TAX'IS (ταξις), *arrangement.*

tac'tics, *the evolution, maneuvers, etc., of military and naval forces; the science or art which relates to these.*

tacti'cian, *one skilled in tactics.*

syn'tax, *the arrangement of words into sentences.*

syntac'tical, *relating to syntax.*

tax'idermy (Gr. n. *der'ma*, skin), *the art of preparing and arranging the skins of animals in their natural appearance.*

tax'idermist, *one skilled in taxidermy.*

32. TECH'NE (τεχνη), *art.*

tech'nical, *relating to an art or profession.*

technical'ity, *a technical expression; that which is technical.*

technol'ogy, *a treatise on or description of the arts.*

technol'ogist, *one skilled in technology.*

polytech'nic (Gr. adj. *pol'us*, many), *comprising many arts.*

pyr'otechny (Gr. n. *pur*, fire), *the art of making fireworks.*

33. THE'OS (θεος), *God.*

the'ism, *belief in the existence of a God.*

theo'cracy. (See *kratos.*)

theo'logy. (See *logos.*)

apotheo'sis, *glorification, deification.*

a'theism, *disbelief in the existence of God.*

a'theist, *one who does not believe in the existence of God.*

enthu'siasm, *heat of imagination; ardent zeal.*

pan'theism. (See *pan.*)

pol'ytheism (Gr. adj. *polus*, many), *the doctrine of a plurality of Gods.*

34. TITH'ENI (τιθεναι), *to place, to set.*

theme, *a subject set forth for discussion.*

the'sis, *a proposition set forth for discussion.*

anath'ema, *an ecclesiastical curse.*

antithesis, *opposition or contrast in words or deeds.*

hypoth'esis, *a supposition.*

paren'thesis, *something inserted in a sentence which is complete without it.*

syn'thesis, *a putting together, as opposed to analysis.*

35. TON'OS (τονος), *tension, tone.*

tone, *tension, vigor, sound.*

ton'ic, adj. *increasing tension or vigor*; n. *a medicine which increases strength.*

tune, *a series of musical notes on a particular key.*

attune', *to make musical; to make one sound agree with another.*

bar'ytone (Gr. adj. *ba'rus*, heavy), *a male voice.*

diaton'ic, *proceeding by tones and semitones.*

in'tonate, *to sound; to modulate the voice.*

intone', *to give forth a slow, protracted sound.*

sem'itone, *half a tone.*

REVIEW EXERCISE ON GREEK DERIVATIVES.

1. Derivation of "antithesis"?—Compose an example of an antithesis.—Point out the antithesis in the following:—

> "The prodigal robs his heir; the miser robs himself."
> "A wit with dunces and a dunce with wits."
> "Though deep, yet clear, though gentle, yet not dull,
> Strong without rage, without o'erflowing, full."

2. Derivation of "hypothesis."—Give an adjective formed from this noun.—What Latin derivative corresponds literally to "hypothesis"? *Ans. Supposition.*—Show this. *Ans.* Supposition is composed of sub = hypo (under), and position (from *ponere,* to place) = thesis, a placing—What adjective from "supposition" would correspond to "hypothetical"? *Ans. Supposititious.*

3. Derivation of "parenthesis"?—Compose a parenthetical sentence.

4. What is the opposite of "synthesis"?—Give the distinction *Ans. Analysis* is taking apart, *synthesis* is putting together—What adjective is derived from the noun "synthesis"?

5. What adjective is formed from "demagogue"? *Ans. Demagogic* or *demagogical*—Define it—Compose a sentence containing the word "demagogue". MODEL: "Aaron Burr, to gain popularity, practiced the arts of a *demagogue*."

6. What adjective is formed from "pedagogue"? *Ans. Pedagogic*—What would the "*pedagogic* art" mean?—Is "pedagogue" usually employed in a complimentary sense?—Give a synonym of "pedagogue" in its literal sense.

7. Derivation of "anarchy"?—Compose a sentence containing this word. MODEL: "Many of the South American States have long been cursed by *anarchy*."

8. What adjective is formed from "monarchy"? *Ans. Monarchical*—Define it.—Can you mention a country at present ruled by a monarchical government?—What is the ruler of a monarchy called?

9. Compose a sentence containing the word "oligarchy". MODEL: "During the Middle Ages some of the Italian republics, as Genoa and Venice, were under the rule of an *oligarchy*."

10. From what root is "democracy" derived?—What adjective is formed from "democracy"?—Is Russia at present a *democracy*?—Can you mention any ancient governments that for a time were democracies?

11. What adjective is formed fiom "aristocracy"?—What noun will denote one who believes in aristocracy? *Ans. Aristocrat*—What does "aristocrat" ordinarily mean? *Ans.* A proud or haughty person who holds himself above the common people.

12. What is the etymology of "thermometer"?

13. Illustrate the meaning of "chronometer" by using it in a sentence.

14. What adjective is formed from "diameter"? *Ans. Diametrical*—What adverb is formed from "diametrical"?—What is meant by the expression "*diametrically* opposed"?

15. What science was the forerunner of astronomy? *Ans. Astrology*—Give the derivative of this word.—What word denotes one who is skilled in astronomy?—Form an adjective from "astronomy."—Compose a sentence containing the word "astronomy." MODEL: "The three great founders of *astronomy* are Copernicus, Kepler, and Newton."

16. From what root is "telescope" derived?—Combine and define telescop + ic.—Compose a sentence using the word "telescope."

17. From what root is "microscope" derived?—Combine and define microscop + ic.—What single word denotes microscopic animals? *Ans. Animalculæ.*—Compose a sentence containing the word "microscope." MODEL: "As the telescope reveals the infinitely distant, so the *microscope* reveals the infinitely little."

18. Compose a sentence containing the word "antipathy." MODEL: "That we sometimes have antipathies which we cannot explain is well illustrated in the lines:

> 'The reason why I cannot tell,
> I do not like you, Dr. Fell.'"

19. What adjective is formed from "apathy"?

20. Derivation of "sympathy"?—Give a synonym of this Greek derivative. *Ans. Compassion.*—Show why they are literal synonyms. *Ans.* Sym = con or com, and pathy = passion; hence, compassion = sympathy.—Give an English derivative expressing the same thing. *Ans. Fellow-feeling.*

21. From what two roots is "autocrat" derived?—Form an adjective from "autocrat."—Who is the present "autocrat of all the Russias"?—Could the Queen of England be called an *autocrat*?—Why not?

22. Compose a sentence containing the word "autograph." MODEL: "There are only two or three *autographs* of Shakespeare in existence."

23. Derivation of "automaton"?—Illustrate the signification of the word by a sentence.

24. What word would denote a remedy for "all the ills that flesh is heir to"? —Compose a sentence containing the word "panacea."

25. Derivation of "panoply"?—In the following sentence is "panoply" used in a literal or a figurative sense? "We had need to take the Christian *panoply*, to put on the whole armor of God."

26. From what two roots is "pantheism" derived?—What word is used to denote one who believes in pantheism?

27. Can you mention an ancient religion in which there were many gods?— Each divinity might have its own temple; but what name would designate a temple dedicated to *all* the gods?

28. Give an adjective formed from the word "panorama."—Compose a sentence using the word "panorama."

9 781835 521069

Printed by BoD™in Norderstedt, Germany